Cambridge Elements ≡

Elements in Religion and Monotheism
edited by
Paul K. Moser
Loyola University Chicago
Chad Meister
Bethel University

MONOTHEISM AND HOPE IN GOD

William J. Wainwright
University of Wisconsin

CAMBRIDGE
UNIVERSITY PRESS

CAMBRIDGE
UNIVERSITY PRESS

University Printing House, Cambridge CB2 8BS, United Kingdom

One Liberty Plaza, 20th Floor, New York, NY 10006, USA

477 Williamstown Road, Port Melbourne, VIC 3207, Australia

314–321, 3rd Floor, Plot 3, Splendor Forum, Jasola District Centre,
New Delhi – 110025, India

79 Anson Road, #06–04/06, Singapore 079906

Cambridge University Press is part of the University of Cambridge.

It furthers the University's mission by disseminating knowledge in the pursuit of
education, learning, and research at the highest international levels of excellence.

www.cambridge.org
Information on this title: www.cambridge.org/9781108708098
DOI: 10.1017/9781108761376

First published 2020

A catalogue record for this publication is available from the British Library.

ISBN 978-1-108-70809-8 Paperback
ISSN 2631-3014 (online)
ISSN 2631-3006 (print)

Monotheism and Hope in God

Elements in Religion and Monotheism

DOI: 10.1017/9781108761376
First published online: August 2020

William J. Wainwright
University of Wisconsin

Author for correspondence: William J. Wainwright, Wjwain@uwm.edu

Abstract: This Element examines aspects of monotheism and hope. Distinguishing monotheism from various forms of nontheistic religions, it explores how God transcends the terms used to describe the religious ultimate. The discussion then turns to the nature of hope and examines how the concept has been used by Augustine, Aquinas, Kierkegaard, and Moltmann, among others. The Christian tradition to which these monotheists belong associates hope and faith with love. In the final section, Wainwright shows the varieties of this kind of love in Islam, Christianity, and theistic Hinduism, and defends the sort of love valorized by them against some charges against it. He examines why the loves prized in these traditions are imperfect because their adherents invariably believe that the love that *they* cherish is superior to that cherished by others.

Keywords: monotheism, hope, love, faith

ISBNs: 9781108708098 (PB), 9781108761376 (OC)
ISSNs: 2631-3014 (online), 2631-3006 (print)

Contents

1 Monotheism and Hope   1

2 Role and Nature of Hope in the Monotheistic Religions   12

3 Love, Hope, and Religious Disagreement   20

   Bibliography   41

1 Monotheism and Hope

Paul Tillich believed that the essence of religious attitudes is "ultimate concern." Ultimate concern is "total." Its object is experienced as numinous or holy, distinct from all profane and ordinary realities. It is also experienced as overwhelmingly real and valuable – indeed, so real and so valuable that, in comparison, all other things appear empty and worthless. As such, it demands total surrender and promises total fulfillment.

These attitudes seem fully appropriate only if their object is maximally great – so perfect and splendid that nothing greater is conceivable. And indeed, Paul J. Griffiths has argued that "if there are any transcultural universals in the sphere of religious thinking, it is probable that . . . the attempt to characterize, delineate, and, if possible . . . exhaustively define maximal greatness" is "among them" (Griffiths 1994, 59). The nature of maximal perfection is controversial, however.

For one thing, the *form* a religious community's ultimate concern takes (and the conception of its object with which it is bound up) varies from one religious community to another. Ultimate concern may take the form of worship and involve praise, love, gratitude, supplication, confession, petition, and the like. But it can also take the form of a quest for the ultimate good. The object of the quest is an existentially appropriated knowledge of the ultimate good or a union with it that transforms us and overcomes our wrongness. The two forms of ultimate concern may be combined or may exist separately. Christianity and theistic Hinduism combine both. In Theravada Buddhism and Taoism, on the other hand, ultimate concern typically takes the second form but not the first.

In practice, a religious community's conception of the divine is largely determined by its conviction that the object of its devotion is maximally great, by the spoken or oral texts it regards as authoritative, and by metaphysical assumptions and valuations widely shared by the community's members. Of course, these sources aren't independent of one another. The form that ultimate concern takes in a community *incorporates* its most fundamental evaluations, and the authoritative texts that express and shape its ultimate concern present pictures of the world and our place in it that include explicit or implicit metaphysical claims. The Buddhist's picture, for example, expresses the vision of a world in constant flux – devoid of fixity or any kind of permanent substance.

Since the form that ultimate concern takes, the texts regarded as authoritative, and the metaphysical assumptions and evaluations inextricably bound up with these forms and texts vary from one religious community to another, it is hardly surprising that conceptions of maximal greatness vary as well.

The most striking disagreement is between those who regard the divine reality as personal and those who do not. Theists believe that even though the object of their ultimate concern transcends all finite realities, it is more like a person than anything else with which we are ordinarily familiar, and they typically conceptualize it as a maximally perfect person. Persons are rational agents, however – beings who have beliefs about themselves and act on the basis of them. The major theistic traditions have therefore described ultimate reality as an omniscient mind and omnipotent will. Other religious traditions are nontheistic. Advaita Vedanta and Theravada Buddhism are examples.

Advaita Vedanta's rejection of theism is a consequence of its insistence that "Brahman [ultimate reality] is without parts or attributes ... one without a second" (Shankara [traditional attribution] second half of the eighth century, 101). If the Brahman has *no* properties, it necessarily lacks the properties of omniscience, perfect goodness, omnipotence, and personhood, and cannot therefore be understood as God.

The rejection also follows from Advaita's conviction that Brahman contains no internal diversity ("is without parts") and is identical with the whole of reality ("is one without a second"). If the Brahman is all there is, for example, then there is nothing outside Brahman that could serve as an object of its knowledge. And if it is devoid of internal diversity, there can be no self-knowledge either, for self-knowledge involves an internal differentiation between the self as knower and the self as known. Nor can the Brahman be a causal agent. If the Brahman is maximally perfect, it must be unlimited. But it *is* limited if something exists outside it. The Brahman must therefore be all there is. If the Brahman is identical with the whole of reality, though, and Brahman contains no plurality, then reality as a whole is an undifferentiated unity. The space-time world with its distinctions between times, places, and events is consequently unreal. *Real* causal relations are relations between two real things, however. So Brahman is neither the cause of the space-time world as a whole nor of the events in it, and is thus neither the space-time world's creator nor its ruler. It follows from these considerations that Brahman is neither an omniscient mind nor an omnipotent and active will. It cannot be a maximally perfect *person*, therefore, and so can be *God*.[1]

---

[1] Advaita does contain what might be called "theistic elements." For example, it distinguishes the nirguna from the saguna Brahman. The former is the Brahman without attributes. The latter is the Brahman with attributes and is roughly described in the way that theists describe God. The nirguna Brahman is the Brahman as it really is, however, while the saguna Brahman is ultimately illusory. Yet even though Advaita believes that, like all conceptualizations of the Brahman, the idea of an omnipotent, omniscient, and all-good cause of the space-time world is ultimately false, it regards it as superior to other conceptualizations. Furthermore, Advaita describes the real Brahman as an infinite, joyous consciousness (albeit a consciousness that has no objects or

Some nontheistic religions are totally devoid of elements even remotely resembling theism. According to Theravada Buddhism, for example, a person is simply a collection of interrelated experiences and body states called "dharmas." The dharmas are causally conditioned and transient. (They last for at most a few moments.) Furthermore, the realm of the transient and causally conditioned is the realm of suffering or unsatisfactoriness (duhkha). One cannot therefore construe maximally perfect reality as a person. To do so would imply that it was impermanent, causally conditioned, and unhappy. Ultimate reality (nirvana) is not conscious and it does not act. It is more like a transcendent place or state than a transcendent person.

Other examples of nontheistic ultimates are provided by the Emptiness traditions of Zen and Madhyamika Buddhism, the Daosim of Lao Tzu, and the Neo-Confucianism of Wang Yangmin.

Monotheism

Monotheists think that God is not only personal but the unique source of created being who possesses an omnipotent and all-sovereign will, and is the only proper object of total devotion. Monotheism needn't entail that there aren't any other so-called gods, however. While the Vaishnavism of Ramanuja's and Madhva's Vedanta and the Shaivism of Shaiva Siddhanta are clearly monotheistic, they don't deny the existence of the other gods of Hindu mythology. The Vaishnavas, for instance, downgrade the importance of Indra, Brahma, Shiva, and the other deities. They are *creatures*, called into being by Vishnu, who act as his servants. They thus have more or less the same status as angels in the Jewish, Christian, and Islamic traditions.

Moreover, while some self-proclaimed monotheisms have been accused of polytheism, the accusation is arguably unjustified. Kabbalistic Judaism, Christianity, and the Vaishnavism of theistic Vedanta are examples. None of them posit the existence of independent sources of the whole of creation, independent omnipotent and sovereign wills, or distinct and independent objects of total devotion.

First consider the Kabbalah. The *Zohar* (after 1275) identifies the first principle with the En Sof or infinite (unlimited). The En Sof is "the hidden God" or "innermost being" of God, without attributes or qualities. Because it

---

contents and is thus "empty"). Because Advaita refuses to ascribe either knowledge or activity to ultimate reality, though, it is essentially nontheistic. Its maximally perfect reality isn't the God of the theistic traditions – all-powerful, all-knowing, all-good, the sovereign lord of heaven and earth. It is instead an "infinite ocean" of joyous empty consciousness – impersonal, inactive, and anonymous.

lacks attributes, the En Sof is incomprehensible and thus, in a strict sense, nonpersonal (although it reveals itself as personal).

The hidden God manifests itself in the sefirot, however. These are conceived as God's attributes, or as divine spheres or realms, or as stages (in his self-manifestation). They are also regarded as names that God gives himself, and together form his "one great name"; or as God's faces or garments; or as beams of his light. They are also sometimes pictured as the branches of a tree whose root is the En Sof, "the hidden root of roots." (Alternatively, the En Sof is depicted as the sap that circulates through the branches and maintains them.) The branches are thought of as extending through the whole of the created order; created things exist solely in virtue of the fact that "the power of the sefirot lives and acts in them."

There are ten sefirot or stages in God's self-manifestation. A brief discussion of the first three will be sufficient for our purposes. The first is, perhaps surprisingly, characterized as Nothing or the Abyss. (We are said to catch glimpses of it when things alter their form or disappear; when things change or are destroyed. Nothingness or the Abyss becomes "visible" for "a fleeting . . . moment.") This mystical no-thing-ness is God's Supreme Crown.

Both Wisdom and Intelligence emerge or emanate from the Crown. Wisdom is the "ideal thought" of everything that will emerge in creation. The idea exists at this stage in a confused and undifferentiated form, however. Wisdom is sometimes pictured as a fountain that springs out of Nothingness (the Crown) and from which the other sefirot will flow, sometimes as a seed or germ from which everything develops, and sometimes as a point. (The idea behind this last image is that just as the movement of a point generates a line, and the movement of a line generates a surface, so the "movement" of Wisdom [together with the "movement" of Intelligence] generates the other sefirot.) Intelligence is the principle of "individuation and differentiation" and "upholds" what is "folded up" in Wisdom. (If Wisdom is the "confused" or undifferentiated thought of creation, Intelligence is that thought become clear and distinct [Scholem 1946, 207–9, 213–20; Epstein 1959, 236].)

The doctrine of the divine emanations or sefirot might already be thought to compromise God's unity. But matters become still more problematic in an influential treatise that was composed in Provence around 1230 and (falsely) ascribed to Hai Goan.

According to its pseudonymous author, "three hidden lights" are found in the "root of roots" that exists "above the first sefirah" – "the inner primordial light," the "transparent (or ultraclear) light," and "the clear light." These "lights" are one thing and one substance that "are found without separation and without union, in the most intimate relation with the root of roots" or (more strongly) are the very "name and substance of the root of all roots." The three lights are the immediate source of "the three supreme sefirot of 'Pure Thought,' 'Knowledge,' and 'Intellect,'" but whereas the sefirot "themselves are clearly created [or emanated?] … the triad of the lights illuminate one another, uncreated [and unemanated?] without beginning in the hidden root." According to Pseudo-Hai, then, a triad exists *in the hidden Godhead itself.*

Later Kabbalists were aware "of a possible connection between these ideas and the Christian Trinity," but explained the latter as a corruption of the former. Jesus and his disciples were themselves "real Kabbalists, 'only their Kabbalah was full of mistakes'" – their doctrine of the Trinity was the result of a misinterpretation of the doctrine of the three lights! Whatever one thinks of this, there *are* striking similarities between the two doctrines. But there are also important differences. The lights "are neither persons nor 'hypostases' in God," for example, and there is no mention of "specific relationships" between them (such as begetting and being begotten), or "spiration" and "procession" (Scholem 1987, 349–54).

The suspicion of Christian influence was by no means restricted to the Pseudo-Hai's doctrine of the three lights, however, for "philosophical opponents of the Kabbalah" had already suggested "that the doctrine of the ten sefirot was [itself] of Christian origin" (Scholem 1987, 354). Nor was this criticism easily laid to rest. Thus Isaac bar Sheshet Parfat (1326–1408) says that he had "heard a philosopher speak in a defaming manner of the Kabbalists," saying, "'The Gentiles [Christians] are believers in a trinity, and the Kabbalists are believers in a ten-ity'" (Gellman 2013, 46).

The general problem, of course, was that on its surface at least, the doctrine of the sefirot seems incompatible with "God's unity." Rabbi Azriel of Gerona (d. 1238) addressed this issue in his "Explanation of the Ten Sefirot." In the first place, the higher sefirot, at least, have always existed "in potentia *in* the Eyn Sof before they were actualized" (Azriel 1986, 93, my emphasis). Moreover, because "the receptor [the sefirah] … unite[s] with the bestower [ultimately, the En Sof] in one power … the two are really one." So the answer to our difficulty is apparently this. The emanation of the sefirot is compatible with God's unity because (unlike created beings) the sefirot are contained within the En Sof in a potential or undifferentiated form and because (since their power is the power of the En Sof) there is ultimately only one power. Thus, "no emanation is radiated forth except to proclaim the unity with the Eyn Sof" (Azriel 1986, 93–5). Or as Rabbi Moshe Haim Luzzatto claimed in the first half of the eighteenth century, "the sefirot are not separate from the one who emanates, for they are like the flame connected to the coal; and all is one, a unity that has within it no division" (Gellman 2013, 46). Whether considerations like these fully resolve the problem is a moot question, of course.

Still, the Kabbalah is only one strand within Judaism. By contrast, the doctrine of the Trinity and the divinity of both Vishnu and his consort Lakshmi are firmly rooted at the very heart of Christianity and Shri Vaishnavism respectively. Perhaps as a result, these traditions have devoted much more thought to reconciling monotheism with elements that, on their face, seem at odds with it.

Christians are not tritheists, for they do not regard the Father, Son, and Holy Spirit as three distinct gods. The Western or Augustinian tradition, for example, does not think there are three distinct powers, intellects, or wills since, in its view, the divine power, intellect, and will are aspects of a single divine essence that subsists in three "persons" or "hypostases."

Another view, though, is implicit in the position of many second- and third-century church fathers, some western Christian Platonists, and the Eastern Orthodox Church as a whole. The Trinitarian views of Ralph Cudworth (1617–88) are fairly typical of this position. There are three hypostases or "persons." Each has its own individual essence. But all share a common generic essence (namely, divinity), so that each member of the Trinity is eternal, necessarily existent, omnipotent, omniscient, perfectly good, and the like.

"There is not a trinity of [independent] principles," however, "but ... only one principle or fountain of Godhead [the Father] ... from which the other[s, namely, the Son and the Holy Spirit] are derived." They together constitute one entity ("one entire divinity"), as "the root, and the stock and the branches" constitute "one tree," or as the sun, the light, and its splendor are "undivided" and form one thing. Indeed, there is so "near a conjunction" between the Father, Son, and Holy Spirit as can be found nowhere else in nature. The relations between them are necessary and eternal; they are "indivisibly and inseparably united." Moreover, each person inheres or indwells in the others, and they are all "*ad extra* one and the same God, jointly concurring in all the same actions," being all "one creator" (Cudworth 1678, 598, 616–20).

Nor is each member, in abstraction from the others, an appropriate object of total devotion and unconditional commitment. In spite of the aberrations of some Christians, it is reasonably clear that the object of the Christian's ultimate concern is the Trinity *as a whole*, and not one or more of its members considered in isolation. Christian attitudes toward the Father, for example, are inseparable from Christian attitudes toward the Son. Christ is worshiped *as* the Son of the Father, for instance, and the Father is worshiped *as* the one who fully reveals himself in Christ.

The Shri Vaishnavas provide another example of a monotheism that is "tainted" by elements that appear to be in tension with it. Their picture of reality is clearly monotheistic. Problems are created, however, by the fact that the scriptures on which the Shri Vaishnavas draw closely associate Vishnu with his consort Lakshmi. In the *Pancaratras*, for example, "the five functions associated with God's oversight of the world," namely, creation, preservation, destruction, and "obscuration" and "favoring" (roughly, withholding and bestowing grace) are sometimes ascribed to Vishnu and sometimes to Lakshmi (Kumar 1997, 23–4). Again, while Ramanuja and his great predecessor, Yamuna, have little or nothing to say about Lakshmi in their philosophical writings, she plays a significant role in their devotional works, which describe her as the mediatrix between Vishnu and his devotees. Yamuna described her as inseparable from the Lord, for example, and insists that while nonintelligent and intelligent beings (including the gods such as Brahma and Shiva) are "only a small part of God's reality, . . . the divine consort" is "the equal match of the Lord, . . . sharing the same auspicious qualities" (Kumar 1997, 61). Ramanuja, too, claims that Vishnu and Lakshmi are "eternally associated" and asserts that both possess "the multitude . . . of unlimited, unsurpassed, and innumerable auspicious qualities" (Kumar 1997, 66–7). All of this is regarded as compatible with the oneness or nonduality of God. The precise relationship between Vishnu and Lakshmi was left undefined, however, and it remained for later generations to work out fuller accounts that both respected Lakshmi's importance to ritual and devotion and at the same time protected monotheism. There were two major resolutions.

The first is represented by Lokacarya (1213–1323). For Lokacarya, the divine consort's role is subordinate and, perhaps, ultimately nonessential. Lakshmi "displays the three essential attributes of a mediator: mercy . . ., dependence on the Lord [Vishnu], . . . and nonsubservience [to] another [than the Lord]." Her ability to mediate between the souls and their Lord is thus ultimately dependent upon Vishnu. In other words, Shri Lakshmi "mediates not as an equal partner of the Lord . . . but only as his dependent and subordinate." There is even a suggestion that Vishnu can himself function as a mediator without Lakshmi's existence. Thus Lokacarya "points out that in the *Mahabharata*, Krishna himself becomes the mediator, whereas in the *Ramayana*, Sita becomes the mediator." (The relevance of this remark becomes clear when one recalls that both Krishna and Sita's consort, Rama, are avataras or "descents" [very roughly, incarnations] of Vishnu [Kumar 1997, 102–7].) Lokacarya, then, preserves monotheism by more or less downgrading Lakshmi's status.

Venkatanatha (1268–1369) offers a different solution. He does distinguish "the two [salvific] functions of the Lord and his consort," the Lord being "depicted as the father who disciplines the sinner," and Lakshmi as the divine mother who intercedes for him. The distinction between these two functions is not absolute, however, for the divine consort merely "bring[s] out 'the Lord's natural compassion' so that that compassion becomes the basis for the spiritual rebirth of the offending devotee" (Kumar 1997, 120–1). Moreover, (and most important) there is no real or ontological difference between the divine father and the divine mother. Lakshmi is an inseparable attribute of Vishnu. Since a substance and its inseparable attributes "share in the same essential nature," and since one can't understand a substance without understanding its "essential and inseparable attribute[s]," the Lord and his divine consort form "a single reality" (Kumar 1997, 146–7). Thus "whenever Bhagavan [i.e., Vishnu] is referred to, Lakshmi should also be considered as referred to," and when one offers oneself to either, one is offering oneself to both since the deity to which one offers oneself "is single [though] it rests with two" (Kumar 1997, 124). Venkatanatha thus preserves monotheism by denying that God and his divine consort are ontologically distinct.

The Transcendence of God

There is little doubt that the appeal to and adoration of mystery is a characteristic feature of much Christian thought and practice. Pseudo-Dionysius, for example, begins his *Mystical Theology* by asking the Trinity to guide him to the "most exalted" and hidden secrets of Scripture, which "exceedeth light and more than exceedeth knowledge, where ... the mysteries of heavenly truth lie hidden in the dazzling obscurity of the secret silence outshining all brilliance with the intensity of their darkness" (Dionysius 1957, 191). Nor are themes like this peculiar to Christian mystics and mystical theologians. They are commonplace in the Church Fathers and in a number of later Christian theologians.

Consider first John Chrysostom.

> St. Paul said: "The Lord ... dwells in unapproachable light." And pay heed to the accuracy with which Paul speaks ... He does not say: "Who dwells in incomprehensible light," but "in unapproachable light," and this is much stronger than "incomprehensible." A thing is said to be incomprehensible when those who seek after it fail to comprehend it, even after they have searched and sought to understand it, but it does not elude all inquiry and questioning. A thing is unapproachable which, from the start, cannot be investigated nor can anyone come near to it. [Yet] suppose ... we forget Paul and the prophets for a moment, [and] mount up to the heavens ... Do you think that the angels in heaven talk over and ask each other questions about the divine essence? By no means! What are the angels doing? They give glory to God and they adore him, they chant without ceasing their triumphal and

mystical hymns with a deep feeling of religious awe. Some sing: "Glory to God in the highest"; the seraphim chant: "Holy, holy, holy," and they turn away their eyes because they cannot endure God's presence as he comes down to adapt himself to them in condescension. (Chrysostom 1984, 100)

In *Proslogion 15*, Anselm exclaims: "Lord not only are you that than which a greater cannot be thought, but you are also something greater than can be thought. For since it is possible to think that there is such a one, if you were not this same being something greater than you could be thought – which cannot be" (Anselm 1965, 137).

Commenting on this passage, M. J. Charlesworth observes that Anselm is reminding us that "even if we understand God to be 'that than which nothing greater can be thought,' we do not thereby have a *positive* or *determinate* knowledge of God" (Anselm 1965, 81, my emphases), and refers us to the reply to Gaunilo where Anselm says that just as one can think or understand "the ineffable" though one can't "specify [or describe] what is said to be ineffable; and just as one can think of [or understand] the inconceivable – although one cannot think of what 'inconceivable' applies to – so also 'that than which a greater cannot be thought' ... can be thought of and understood even if the thing itself cannot be thought or understood" (Anselm 1965, 189).

Aquinas says that "since our mind is not proportionate to the divine substance, that which is the substance of God remains beyond our intellect and so is unknown to us. Hence the supreme knowledge which man has of God is to know that he does not know God, in so far as he knows that what God is surpasses all that we can understand of him" (*de Potentia*, q. 7 a 5, quoted in Rahner 1974, 58–9). Karl Rahner seems to me to be correct in arguing that, because "the reason for saying" that knowing God involves knowing that one does not know God "holds good for the beatific vision" as well as for the veiled glimpses of God we have in this life, "there is no reason for not applying it to the knowledge of God in the beatific vision" (Rahner 1974, 59).

One of the most powerful statements of this view is given by John Chrysostom, who exclaims: "let us call upon him, then, as the ineffable God who is beyond intelligence, invisible, incomprehensible. Let us call on him as the God who is inscrutable to the angels, unseen by the Seraphim, inconceivable to the cherubim, invisible to the principalities, to the powers, and to the virtues, in fact to *all* creatures without qualification because he is known *only* by the Son and the Spirit" (Chrysostom 1984, 97, my emphases). Why do the seraphim "stretch forth their wings and cover their faces? For what other reason than they cannot endure the sparkling flashes nor the lightning which shines from the throne. Yet they did not see the pure light itself nor the pure essence itself. What they saw was a condescension accommodated to their nature,"

Chrysostom 1984, 101). So unless the beatified see God more clearly than the angels do, even they do not grasp God's essence! The mystery of God is thus ineluctable.

Nor are appeals to mystery peculiar to Christian worship and reflection. Maimonides believed that God can only be described negatively, and the Kabbalists thought that while "the God of religion" has many names, "the *deus absconditus*, the God who is hidden in his own self, can only be named ... with the help of words ... which are not real names at all ... The early Spanish Kabbalists," for example, used terms like "'Great Reality,' 'Indifferent Unity,' and above all En Sof [the infinite]." Isaac the Blind called the hidden God "that which is not conceivable by thinking," and thus not "He who is not, etc." (Scholem 1946, 11–12).

But if God is an ineluctable mystery as Chrysostom, Anselm, Maimonides, and others maintain, then he can't be caught in our conceptual webs. While we can perhaps say what God is not, and deploy symbols, analogies, and the like to express the divine mystery, no positive statement about God is literally true. Yet if that is the case, theists must qualify the claim that God is a person. While God may be analogous to persons in certain respects, and personhood may be an appropriate metaphor or symbol for the God of the Hebrew Bible or of the New Testament, for Allah, for the Vishnu of Ramanuja or Madhva, or for the Shiva of Shiva Siddhanta, God is not literally a person. Only a few contemporary evangelicals believe *that*.

But neither are William Alston, William Rowe, and others clearly correct in saying that "a symbolic or metaphorical statement S is [cognitively] meaningful only if what it expresses can be replaced by some [cognitively] meaningful literal statement S*" (Rowe 1968, 137). If there were some positive literally true statements about God, in their view, we could use those statements to determine which symbolic or metaphorical or analogical statements about God approach the truth more closely than others do. In their absence, however, while symbols, metaphors, or analogies might somehow *point* to God, they don't increase our understanding of him.

This commonly accepted view is arguably mistaken, however. For one thing, poetry seems to provide counterexamples. Shakespeare's *Romeo and Juliet*, for instance, expresses what young love is like better than any set of literal statements could.[2] A more important point, though, is this.

---

[2] An anonymous reader has correctly pointed out that the play arguably includes "actual claims" about "[the nature of] young love." But while it is true that we can learn various facts about young love from the play, it doesn't follow that we can therefore *feel* or vicariously *experience* what young love is like. Arguably the *poetry* of the play can sometimes make this possible.

While Rowe and others don't clearly distinguish between symbols, metaphors, and analogies, the distinctions between them are crucial. Their criticism rests on the claim that God talk can't be symbolic all the way down, and while this is right, it isn't right for the reasons they give. We *do* need some literally true positive statements about God for our God talk to be cognitively meaningful. But these statements needn't take the form of singling out a property P that S and S* have in common. Cognitively meaningful statements about God need neither assert nor presuppose that God and creatures share identically the same properties. For consider the following two counterexamples.

Analogies of proportionality state that God has a property, P, which stands to him as (e.g.) goodness or personhood stands to us. And, even though "God is a person" isn't literally true, it *is* literally true that God stands to some property, P, as personhood stands to us. Moreover, all properties entailed by (and not merely associated with) goodness or personhood or by other properties ascribed to him by analogies of proportionality, are literally ascribed to him as well – albeit they, too, are understood analogically. (Even though the position in question is usually stated in this way, however, that can't be quite right. For because all statements entail all necessary truths, any analogical statement entails [e.g.] $2 + 2 = 4$. And the latter cannot be understood analogically. We may be able to get around this difficulty, though, by stipulating that only those statements that are entailed by the *content* of our analogical statements [as determined by the content of the analogical *terms* employed in them] are to be understood analogically.)

Likeness statements provide another example. A sentence of the form "x is like y" is, if true at all, literally true. Not all likeness statements are informative, of course. "It isn't helpful to be told that God is like so and so," for example, "since any two things are like each other in some respect" (Alston 1989, 32). But even if this is true in general, *some* literally true likeness statements *are* informative.

Core metaphors are typically (disguised) comparisons. "God is a craftsman," for example, implicitly asserts that God's relation to the world is more like that of the relation of a craftsman to his product than that of a seed to the plant which grows from it, or the sun to the heat and light it emits. In practice, less-favored models are typically drawn from rival religious traditions or doctrinal competitors within one's own tradition. If this is correct, then some metaphorical theological assertions will contradict others. "God is a craftsman" contradicts "God is the world egg or seed" since the first implicitly asserts that God is (*uberhaupt*) more like a craftsman (and hence a person) than a seed, whereas the second implicitly asserts the opposite.[3] If this is correct, then religious metaphors are often equivalent to similes, and similes are likeness statements – statements that if true at all, are literally true. That x is like y, however, doesn't entail that x and y have a common property, P, such that the cognitive content of "x is like y" is more or less equivalent to "x is P."

It is futile to search for a common property (or set of properties) that exhausts the cognitive content of "The sound of a trumpet is like the color scarlet," for example. Or consider "Scarlet is like crimson," or "The taste of oysters is like the taste of clams." We can't specify a common property or set of properties that ground the likeness that scarlet and crimson, or the two tastes, literally have. The two statements are nonetheless literally and informatively true. We can, of course, specify the relevant classes of comparison, namely colors or tastes, or point out that both crimson and scarlet are hues of red. But doing so doesn't explicate the similarities the statements are calling our attention to. Blue and scarlet are also colors, and the taste of oysters and the taste of bananas are also tastes, for example, and while there are many hues of red, the likeness of crimson and scarlet differs from the likeness of hues of red that are further removed from crimson and scarlet on the color scale. The similarity between crimson and scarlet is thus not adequately captured by the fact that both are hues of red.

Furthermore, as these examples indicate, the cognitive content of a simile may be hidden from a person who hasn't experienced both terms of the relevant comparison. A man or woman who hasn't experienced the sound of a trumpet or the color scarlet is not in a position to understand "The sound of a trumpet is like the color scarlet" – let alone recognize its truth. Perhaps, though, theistic mystics who purport to have had experiences of God could use their experiences to determine which metaphorical religious statements are closer to the truth than others. And even if one hasn't had an explicit experience of God oneself, others whom one trusts may have – in which case one's belief that a religious metaphor A is closer to the truth than religious metaphor B might legitimately rest on their authority.

2 Role and Nature of Hope in the Monotheistic Religions

Many contemporary philosophers believe that a combination of two conditions is necessary and sufficient for hope. First, what is hoped for must be strongly

---

[3] Not all religious metaphors are comparative, of course. If a Shakta asserts "God is our mother," his assertion implies that God is more like a mother than a father (or more precisely, more like a mother than the masculine figures of Vishnu or Shiva). But when Julian of Norwich addresses God (or Jesus) as mother, her exclamations imply only that God's (or Jesus's) relation to us is significantly like that of a mother.

desired. And, second, what is desired must be highly improbable, although precisely how improbable is a matter of dispute. There is general agreement that the object of hope must at least be logically possible, but some think it must also be physically possible while others do not. All agree, though, that what is hoped for must have at least some probability, even if that probability is almost vanishingly low.

But while everyone agrees that these conditions are necessary for hope, not everyone thinks they are sufficient. Ariel Meirav, for example, points out that while Mary's and Bob's desire for some occurrence may be equally intense and they may regard its occurrence as equally improbable, Mary may hope for it while Bob despairs of it. What Meirav thinks accounts for this difference is that Mary believes in the existence of a good "external factor" (the existence of God, for instance, or a benevolent nature, or human progress), which, if it obtains, makes hope not unreasonable, and Bob does not (Mierav 2009, 216–33).

Hope's Role in the Monotheistic Religions

While hope in all of the major religious traditions centers around what those traditions regard as a maximally perfect reality, the role that that reality plays differs. God, for example, is the *object* of the theist's hope, but the maximally perfect reality is more often the *ground* of hope in the nontheistic religions. The Nirvana of Theravada Buddhism or the Emptiness of Zen or Madhyamika Buddhism is the ground of hope in those traditions, but what is hoped for is typically the ability to achieve the goals of those traditions by (for example) successfully following the Buddha's Noble Eightfold path, or (in the case of Zen and Madyamika) emptying oneself of conceptualization and attachment, or conforming one's life to the Dao. A major exception to this dichotomy, however, is Pure Land Buddhism, which Paul Williams has characterized as a kind of "devotional monotheism."

Although Pure Land Buddhism had roots in India and central Asia, its richest development occurred in China and Japan. Finding themselves unable to make significant progress toward enlightenment after the most sincere and strenuous efforts to attain it, both monks and laity threw themselves on the mercy of Amitabha (or Amida [Japanese]), the Buddha of the "Western Paradise" (Sukhavati). For Amitabha has promised to bring anyone with sincere faith in him to Sukhavati, where he or she would be instructed in Dharma by Amitabha himself and by Bodhisattvas like Avalokiteshvara who are Amitabha's retainers. Although its beauty is beyond our ability to adequately describe it, it is unsurpassable. Sukhavati is not a "sensuous paradise," however, like the heavens of Hinduism, but a place where the birds "all proclaim the Dharma as do the trees when gently disturbed in the soft breeze" (Williams 1981, 255). One's faith in Amitabha's promises must be "[1] sincere and [2] deep," though, and (3) "accompanied by an overriding desire for rebirth in Sukhavati" (Williams 1981, 255, 261).

Pure Land Buddhism is thus a grace religion, since one's entry to Sukhavati (and hence ultimately enlightenment) depends on Amitabha's "other power" rather than on one's "own power." The distinction between other power and own power is perhaps best illustrated by Pure Land Buddhism's development in Japan. Honen, the founder of the Jodo Shu Pure Land Sect, thought that while one shouldn't commit even the slightest sin, the only practice needed for entry into Sukhavati was the joyful repetition of the Buddha's name (the nembutsu), "always returning thanks for the great blessedness of having come in contact with the original vow of the Amida Buddha" (Williams 1981, 266).

Although Shinran regarded himself as Honen's disciple, his school was eventually distinguished from Honen's and became known as "Jodo Shin Shu – the True Pure Land Sect." Shinran insisted that we can do nothing on our own that is free from egocentricity and hence truly good. Salvation is wholly Amida's gift. In consequence, "we can only have faith because faith" is itself nothing but "a shining forth of our innate Buddha nature which is [Amida] himself ... [W]hen faith arises, and the Buddha nature shines, ... one is already saved" (Williams 1981, 272). While in theory, one's tenure in Sukhavati (where one is instructed in Dharma by Amida and his attendants) is nothing more than a means to enlightenment, in practice it often appears to be an end in itself.

Hope That, Hope In, and Hope *Simpliciter*

"Hope that" should be distinguished from "hope in." I may hope that my granddaughter will recover from her illness, for example, or that the Milwaukee Brewers will win the 2021 World Series, or that world peace will eventually be established, or that Christ will come quickly, or that my father was innocent. By contrast, I hope in something that may or may not be a person. I may place my trust in my trusty sword or my own right arm, for example, or in an environmentally threatened nature's ability to heal itself, or (if I am a theist) in God.

Gabriel Marcel and others have distinguished hope as such from hope in and hope that. Just as desire and attraction are the opposites of fear and repugnance, so hope *simpliciter* is the opposite of despair. Marcel argues that hope as such doesn't have an object. But this may be doubted since, for Marcel, hope in the sense in question is an affirmation of, or openness to Being, and if it is, then it does have an object of sorts.

The Rationality of Religious Hope

"I hope that x" implies that x's occurrence is desirable although uncertain or even improbable. "I hope in x" – in God or nature, for instance, doesn't imply that x is uncertain but only that what I hope from it is. Hope in God or nature is arguably irrational only if it would violate God's will or wishes, or nature's proper development. Nor is hope in God necessarily irrational even if one has strong reasons for doubting his existence. It is arguably not irrational if there is a nonnegligible, albeit low, probability that God exists, the good one seeks is great enough and compatible with God's nature, and one's desire for that good is sufficiently intense.

Whether hope in God is rational is a function of (1) how great the good one hopes to receive from him is; (2) how probable or improbable it is that one will receive that good from God (which is, in turn, a function of the probability that God exists and the probability that he would provide the good one hopes for if he does exist); (3) the intensity of one's desire for the good one hopes for; and (4) the comparative value of the good one hopes for, that is, the degree to which it surpasses or is surpassed by other goods one hopes for.

Arguably if one of the four factors ranks low but the rankings of the other three are sufficiently high, it may still be rational (or at least not irrational) to hope for the good in question. On the other hand, if what one hopes for isn't good at all (the torture and extermination of all one's enemies, for instance, or the satisfaction of one's base desires), then one can't rationally hope for it. Moreover, if what one hopes for is not only a comparatively minor good but its realization is highly improbable, then one's hope for it is dubiously rational at best.

Again, if the probability of securing the good one hopes for is very low and one's desire for it is not only quite weak but lacks a higher-order desire that it be stronger than it is, then it seems (subjectively) irrational[4] to center one's life on it in the way that the theist centers her life on the goods she hopes to receive from God – most notably God himself or a life with God.

The Virtue of Hope in Christian Theology

Christian theologians' accounts of hope are frequently coupled with discussions of faith and charity. Augustine's *Enchiridion* is typical in this respect. He often

---

[4] That is, irrational given what he *actually* believes and wants, the degree to which he *actually* wants it, etc., as distinguished from what he *should* strongly believe, want, and so on.

speaks as if "faith" is synonymous with "belief." Belief's objects can be past, present, or future; good, evil, or neutral. Hope, on the other hand, "is concerned only with good things, with things future, and with things pertaining to the one who purports to have the hope of them." "Faith" is also used in senses other than (mere) belief, however. Scripture, for example, has taught us to identify it with a belief in things that God has proposed for our belief that transcend sensible or intellectual sight. "Saving faith," though, is faith that works "by affection," that is, *by love*. (Augustine 1953, 7, my emphasis). While every form of faith but saving faith can exist without love, hope cannot since one necessarily loves what one hopes for. Moreover, love of God and hope in God entail each other. For a person who truly hopes in God loves God and one who truly loves God hopes in him. Finally, both love of God and hope in God presuppose an affective belief in him.

Charity is greater than either faith or hope, however. "For a man who loves as he ought unquestionably believes and hopes as he ought; whereas he who does not love believes in vain even though the objects of his belief be true, and also hopes in vain, even though the objects of his hope be shown to have reference to the true felicity" (Augustine 1953, 101).

Augustine's view is too narrow, however. Unlike Thomas Aquinas's, for example, it fails to recognize that we can hope for others. In the latter's view the object of a rational creature's hope should be the "infinite good," an "eternal life which consists in the enjoyment of God himself" (Aquinas 1946, vol. 2, 11–11, Q 14. A 2). Because one can't hope for something one believes to be false or impossible, however, hope presupposes faith (belief). Since "the object of faith is a future good, arduous, but possible to attain," we must believe that the good we seek is possible with God's assistance (Aquinas 1946, vol. 2, II-II, Q 17. A 7). The hope of "wayfarers" (those not yet blessed or in heaven) is grounded in a firm belief in the omnipotence and mercy of a God who makes salvation possible (Aquinas 1946, vol. 2, II-II, Q 18, A 4).

Because the "arduous possible good cannot be an object of faith except in so far as it is something future," however, it cannot be an object of faith once it has been attained. It is thus "voided" for the blessed and those in heaven (Aquinas 1946, vol. 2, II-II, Q 18. A 2). Can the blessed or those in heaven hope *for others*, though? The answer is mixed. The blessed can do so but only indirectly. For if one truly loves another, he or she is an alter ego or second self. And if that is the case, then hoping for oneself includes hoping for the other (Aquinas 1946, vol. 2, II-II, Q 17. A 3). (Moreover, in Q 18. A 2, Reply obj. 3, Aquinas argues that those in heaven or the blessed can "hope for the happiness of others . . . yet not by virtue of hope but rather by the love of charity." But this, of course, isn't literally a form of hope in Aquinas's sense but merely an analogue of it.)

A more troublesome difficulty with the standard view, however, is this. An anonymous reviewer has correctly pointed out that "I can hope that something good happened for you last night." So hope is not always directed *toward the future*. I believe that this is correct, but notice that I can only hope that something good happened for my friend yesterday if I don't *know* that it didn't. So hope does at least require the belief that, for all we know, things aren't closed off by the past.

Like Augustine and Aquinas, Søren Kierkegaard, too, believed with Paul that while "faith, hope, and love abide ... the greatest of these is love" (2 Corinthians, 13. 13). For love is "able to undertake the business of the lesser" two "and make them more perfect" (Kierkegaard 1962, 213). Our principal concern in the present section, however, is with love's bearing on hope.

"To relate oneself expectantly to the possibility of the good is to hope, which therefore cannot be some temporal expectancy but rather an *eternal* hope" (Kierkegaard 1962, 134, my emphasis). For what is often called hope in ordinary speech isn't hope at all, but desire or longing, or "longing filled expectancy." In that sense, "hope comes quite easily to the child and youth," and "dwindles away with the years" (Kierkegaard 1962, 239f.).

In Kierkegaard's view, Christian love both believes all things and hopes for all things. It believes, for example, "that love is ... present fundamentally even in the misguided, ... corrupt, ... [and] hateful." It believes, in other words, that every man and woman is lovable, a proper *object* of a true Christian's love as well as a potential *subject* of true love, that is, as a lover. But it also hopes for all things. "Even though love is not apparent, even though the opposite is seen," it presupposes that "love is nonetheless fundamentally present [in the others], and that it will show itself in the deluded, in the misguided, and even in the lost" (Kierkegaard 1962, 209).

"When love believes all things it is not at all" because of "frivolity, inexperience, naiveté, and ignorance .... No, ... Love knows better than anyone else everything that mistrust knows but without being mistrustful" (Kierkegaard 1962, 216). "Through knowledge one only arrives at equilibrium," however, "especially when the art [of acquiring knowledge] is perfectly practiced" (Kierkegaard 1962, 220). Kierkegaard's view is thus partially grounded in a radical scepticism – a belief that reason as such is incapable of discovering decisive reasons for thinking that one existential option is more reasonable than another.

For knowledge, in Kierkegaard's view, is what we are rightfully *fully certain* of. And what we know in this sense is logically compatible with both loving trust and mistrust. The two alternatives are thus placed in equilibrium. "But when a man's knowledge has placed contrasting possibilities in equilibrium and he wants to or has to judge, then what he believes in becomes apparent, who he is, whether he is mistrustful or loving" (Kierkegaard 1962, 218).

What precisely does his choice consist in? It isn't enough for him to act *as if* everyone is lovable and worthy of trust, and it doesn't consist in an exertion of "will power." Rather, he simply finds himself embracing one or the other of the two possibilities.

Yet how is love, and consequently hope, for everyone possible? It is possible because one lives in the God who is love. "He breathes in God; he draws sustenance for his love from God; he is strengthened by God" (Kierkegaard 1962, 229). The highest good is God, and God is love. To love God, therefore, is to love love and hence all those whom God's love embraces, that is, everyone.

Hope is directed toward the future. "But in love to hope all things signifies the lover's relationship to other men, that in relationship to them, hoping for them, he continually keeps possibility open with infinite partiality for his possibility of the good. Consequently, he hopes in love that possibility is present in every moment, that the possibility of the good is present for the other person" (Kierkegaard 1962, 237). And indeed, according to "the lover's understanding, there is even at the last moment the possibility of the good, even for the most lost, therefore still hope." The lover can do this through her "eternal vision of the eternal's appearance in possibility" (Kierkegaard 1962, 240). The opposite of this hope, however, is despair, whether one consciously recognizes that one is in despair or not.

We will conclude this section by examining two comparatively recent and highly influential Christian takes on hope.

Both Glen Tinder (b. 1923) and Jurgen Moltmann (b. 1926) claim that the crucifixion and resurrection of Jesus Christ are the only things making real hope possible.

Tinder, for example, argues that hope in the purely temporal is delusional, for we can't know with any reasonable degree of certainty what the purely temporal future holds in store for us. Moreover, we often find that what we *have* hoped for turns out to have thwarted our hopes. Think, for example, of the actual consequences of attempts to build a paradise on earth – Soviet or Chinese Marxism, for instance, or the French Revolution's Republic. *Real* hope, however, can only be directed toward God, one's true self, and the Kingdom of God, namely, "an all-encompassing and never ending community centered on God," which is "bound together by the mutual love of [all] its members" (Tinder 1999, 43).

God, his kingdom, and one's true self are transcendent realities, however. They can be pointed to or gestured at by metaphors and analogies but ultimately transcend every attempt to capture them in words and concepts. "We hope to see

God in company with our fellow human beings, and we hope to discover our own selves when we do this. But hoping for these things is not like hoping for good weather on a coming day. [For] we can imagine the latter but not the former." True hope, on the other hand, causes us to think of things that, strictly speaking, are unthinkable" (Tinder 1999, 77).

God clearly discloses himself as "deeply and entirely personal," though, if only in a metaphorical or analogical sense. For only a God like that "wholly corresponds with our needs. Once personality has come to light it is seen, under the authority of an irresistible intuition, as morally prior to everything impersonal. Having become cognizant of the personal, the only realities we can think of as valuable beyond measure and therefore as intrinsically ends in themselves, are those we can love and trust, listen to and address." By contrast, impersonal realities like Plato's Idea of the Good, or Aristotle's Unmoved Mover, or Tillich's being itself "are properly at our disposal: we can use them as we please or ignore them" (Tinder 1999, 34–35).[5]

Moltmann claims that "the God of hope" is a God "whom we cannot . . . have in us or over us but always only before us, who encounters us in [his] promises for the future, and whom we therefore . . . can only await in active hope" (Moltmann 1993, 16). Ultimately, our "hope in the promises of God . . . is not a hope in God himself" but a hope "that his future faithfulness will bring . . . the fullness of what he has promised . . . namely, his redeeming and restoring lordship in all things" (Moltmann 1993, 119).

God's promises are unique, however. "The peculiar nature of the Old Testament promises," for example, "can be seen in the fact that they were not liquidated by the history of Israel – neither by disappointment nor by fulfilment – but that on the contrary Israel's experience of history gave them a constantly new and wider interpretation" (Moltmann 1993, 104). With each major event in Israel's history – not only the escape from Egypt, the conquest of Canaan, and the establishment of the kingdom, for example, but also the latter's destruction and the dispersal of its people – faith in God's promises was not abandoned but rather reinterpreted and enlarged.

The destruction of the Kingdom and exile, for instance, were understood as a judgment on Israel. (Though the prophets also insisted that Israel's enemies, too, would be punished.) "But the Prophets' message of judgment nevertheless points to a different future, to a day of Yahweh, which will arise out the night of

---

[5] This is rather dubious, however. It is simply false that we can always ignore or dispose of nonpersonal realities as we please. A hurricane or flood or forest fire are nonpersonal, for example, but when confronted with them, we can't simply ignore them or dispose of them as we please. Similarly, Advaita Vedanta's *nirguna Brahman*, while nonpersonal, couldn't be ignored if it were truly experienced.

judgment." It thus "paves the way" for a vision of "an unheard of new salvation that is on the way, of a new covenant, of the coming glory in [God's] sovereignty over all the earth, and not only for Israel" but for all the nations who will share in God's blessings.

Moreover, the promise is not only "universalized" in its extension of the blessings of Yahweh's lordship to all people, it is also enlarged to include "a conquest of dying and death" (Moltmann 1993, 129, 132).

A specifically "*Christian* eschatology" is new, however, for it "sets out from a definite reality in history," namely Christ's crucifixion and resurrection, and speaks of "*his* future" (Moltmann 1993, 16–7, my emphases). What is hoped for is no longer simply the fulfilment of God's promises in general but the promises that have been made in the Christ events.

Faith in these promises doesn't lead to a retreat from the world, however, but to a "hopeful outgoing *into* the world [my emphasis] . . . by accepting the cross, the suffering and the death of Christ, by taking upon on it the trials and struggles of obedience in the body and surrendering itself to the pain of love." A person who believes in the Christian promises "proclaims in the everyday world the future of the resurrection, of life and the righteousness of God" (Moltmann 1993, 163).

Neither Tinder nor Moltmann professes to have proofs that would convince most intelligent, open-minded, and sufficiently educated persons of the claim that "our main source of hope today, and indeed in all times, is Jesus Christ" (Tinder 1991, 1). Moltmann, for example, clearly thinks that attempts to establish the reality of the Christ events by employing the standards of contemporary historiography are not only bound to fail, they misunderstand what belief in them rests upon, namely, the apostles' *experience* of the crucifixion of Jesus, closely followed by *experiences* (visions, auditions, and the like) of a resurrected Christ (Moltmann 1993, 173f, 180, 197–9).

Even if one finds Tinder's and Moltmann's claims persuasive, they are bound to seem question-begging to adherents of other faiths. We will discuss the difficulties this creates in Section 3 after exploring the central role love plays not only in Christianity but in most if not all of the other major forms of monotheism as well.[6]

3 Love, Hope, and Religious Disagreement

The monotheist's God is omniscient and omnipotent, aware of our needs and able to help us. Why, though, should God wish to do so? The most common

---

[6] And what do monotheists want to say about the hopes of nontheistic religions such as Zen or Madhyamika? That these religions don't secure what they seek? That what they seek isn't worthwhile? That it isn't as worthwhile as what monotheists valorize? The first is rather clearly false, the second is dubious, and the third begs the question.

answer is because he loves us. (Although whether he loves all of us or only some of us is a matter of dispute.) If God loves us, our hopes aren't in vain. But they are arguably *most* secure if one is caught up in an intimate love relationship with the object of one's devotion.

Love in Hindu, Muslim, and Christian Monotheisms

The Shri Vaishnavas, for example, think that one should model one's life on the companions of Vishnu by playing the role of his servant, friend, or lover. The latter is most important, however.

Among the most perfect expressions of an all-consuming love of God are the Alvars – Vaishnava saints who lived between the seventh and ninth centuries. Their songs at times express the "pangs of separation," and at others the exhilarating joys of union. Separation, for example, is expressed in the following:

> "The Lord is away, and the foster mother pities [her] Mistress who pines for her Lord" and is "unable to endure the length of the night: this child of sinful me [she says], with well-formed teeth, round breasts, and rosy mouth keeps saying 'These fair nights are as eternal [unending] as my desire'"(Dasgupta 1955, vol. 3, 75)

Or again, "Day and Night she knows no sleep: In floods of tears her eyes do swim ... She weeps and reels. 'How without thee can I [endure]?'" (Dasgupta 1955, vol. 3, 79).

The joy of union, on the other hand, is expressed in songs like this:"Blissful Lord, anon, my eyes in floods [of tears] did run. 'Oh what is this?' I asked, 'What marvel this?' The perfect one through friendly days and nights elects with me to e'er remain, to union wooing me, his own to make, nor [ever] let me lone" (Dasgupta 1955, vol. 3, 78).

Dasgupta has argued that the Alvars appear to have been among the first to assume the roles of the companions or lovers of Vishnu's avataras (or "descents").

Eric Lott (Lott 1976, 160–62) explains the concept of the avataras as follows:

(1) They are grounded in God's (Vishnu's) compassion, for the benefit of all, but especially the virtuous.

(2) They have a twofold purpose: God reveals himself in the avataras to make himself accessible and to manifest his beauty and splendor.

(3) They are real, not mere appearances.[7]

---

[7] Though, as Julius Lipner points out, the avataric bodies aren't real in the way in which the flesh of the Christian God's Son is real. For Vishnu's avataric bodies are "phenomenalizations of the supernal form [of Vishnu's celestial body as depicted in statues, paintings, etc.] and are non prakritic in nature." (That is, they are not made of the same kind of "stuff" that spatiotemporal bodies are made of [Lipner 1986, 103].)

(4) They involve no diminishment of God's essential nature. So to perceive one of God's avataras is to perceive God himself.

(This view was more common among Vaishnavas than one might think. Madhva's Dvaita Vedanta provides an interesting example. While some avataras have had more devotional significance than others, their "actual numbers were innumerable" and each was an "essential part of the greater whole that is Vishnu. These [parts] moreover, are not different from the whole. Therefore the avataras are [each] identical with Vishnu as well as with one another" [Sarma 1986, 70].)

There are many stories about Vishnu's avataras and their companions and lovers, and in particular about the two that are arguably most important in the Vaishnava's practice – Rama and Krishna. Thus "King Kula-sekhare who was an alvar and devotee of Rama, used to listen rapturously to the *Ramayana* being recited," and as "he listened . . . became so excited that when he heard of Rama's venturing forth against Ravana," the demon king of Sri Lanka, "he would give orders to mobilize his whole army to march forward to Lanka as an ally of Rama" (Dasgupta 1955, vol. 3, 82). Others assumed the role of the companions of Krishna and most significantly his lovers, the *gopis* or female cowherds who joined him in dance.

The last view was most strikingly expressed by Gaudiya Vaishnavism, which was developed by Caitanya and his followers and went so far as to *identify* ultimate reality with Krishna. In their opinion Krishna is the highest form of God, possessing all beauties and all powers or excellences.[8] Our devotion should therefore be wholly centered on him, and takes two forms.

The first is gauni (secondary) bhakti (love). In this stage, the devotee (e. g.) goes on pilgrimages to the God's shrines, sings songs that praise him, recites prayers to him, listens to scriptures that describe the Lord, constantly thinks of him, worships him in images, recites his names, and so on. Because gauni bhakti is only a preparatory stage, however, these practices aren't ends in themselves. They have no intrinsic value but are simply expressions of our desire to acquire heartfelt love for God, and aids to that acquisition.

The second is para or supreme bhakti. One's heart at this stage is wholly devoted to the Lord. Single-minded ("one-pointed") love of Krishna is attended by ecstatic joy, by visions of the supernal form of God,[9] and by theistic mystical experience that incorporates a sense of ecstatic union with one's beloved.

---

[8] Note that if God's (Vishnu's) avataras express his essential nature without diminishment, it is only a short step to the view that Krishna *is* God.

[9] As depicted in scripture, images, and paintings. As Lipner says in another context, the devotee enjoys "a more or less uninterrupted [and delightful] mental representation of the divine supernal form" which is "so clear and vivid as to be presentational in character" (Lipner 1986, 114–5).

The Gaudiya Vaishnavas who identify ultimate reality with Krishna believe that it is revealed "in the form of a cosmic drama," known as the Krishna-lila. The heart of the drama is the love play between Krishna and the female cowherds or *gopis* whose story is told in the *Bhagavata Purana*. The purpose of the revelation "is to provide humans with a model of, and for, perfection" (Haberman 1988, 45). The model centrally includes a passion that Jiva Gosvamin (fl. 1555–1600) defines as an instance of "that love which consists of an immense desire of a subject for union with the object of its desire," and which Rupa (fl. 1495–1550) claims provides the "highest access" to Krishna (Haberman 1988, 70).

The devotee internalizes the stories of Krishna by identifying with one of Krishna's companions, thereby potentially transforming his or her identity. The anubhavas are the "spontaneous and natural [external] expression" of these characters' "inner emotions." By imitating, or taking on the actions of one of them, the devotee hopes to "obtain the salvific emotions of the character in question, and [thus] come to inhabit the world [namely, *Vraja*[10]] in which that character resides" (Haberman 1988, 69f.)

The five most important are shanta bhava, dasya bhava, sakhya bhava, vatsalya bhava, and madhura bhakti. The first is a "calm or peaceful" awareness of or attraction to God's awful majesty. This is distinguished from love proper but *is* a form of attachment. The second is the attitude of a faithful servant whose love for his master is mixed with reverence and awe. The devotee adopting this attitude toward God looks on himself and behaves as God's privileged servant. While this form of love is more personal than the first, it retains a certain distance between the devotee and the object of his devotion. The last three bhavas become progressively more intimate, however. Sakhya bhava is the attitude of a faithful friend of Krishna. A devotee embracing this role experiences a kind of equality or intimate companionship with his Lord. Vatsalya bhava is the attitude of a mother toward her child and is typified by Krishna's foster mother, Yasoda. Madhura bhaki is the attitude of a young woman toward her lover and is typified by the love of the *gopis* (and most especially, Krishna's favorite *gopi*, Rahda) for their Lord. It is here that the love of God reaches its highest intensity.

To explain more fully: According to Gaudiya Vaishnavism, "the body . . . is the house of the soul or self (*atman*). Identity is what locates the self in a particular body which resides in a particular world. To participate in the world of *Vraja*," for example, "one must occupy a body located in that world.

---

[10] *Vraja* is "the geographic sacred region . . . that is known for the divine acts of Krishna," and is located about 80 miles south of New Delhi. "The earthly *Vraja* also has its corresponding eternal *Vraja* located in the highest heaven" (Schweig, 2014, 169, fn.).

And to accomplish this one must develop an identity which connects one to such a body ... Salvation in Gaudiya Vaishnavism" should therefore "be seen as a shift in identity from the external ... body" of ordinary life "to one's true body which is similar" to that of the exemplary character whose actions one is imitating (Haberman 1988, 73).

Since "amorous emotion (Madhura bhava) contains the essence of all other emotions," it "is perfectly represented by the female lovers of Krishna, ... the *gopis* of *Vraja*." It is "divided into two types." The first involves a "desire for the direct enjoyment" of a union with Krishna. The second involves a "desire to share in the special emotions" of one of the female companions or attendants of his lovers (usually a companion of Radha, Krishna's favorite *gopi*) and thus to vicariously share in the latter's amorous passion (Haberman 1988, 81–5).

Love is also central to Sufism. Rabi'a, for example, was "that one set apart in the seclusion of holiness, that woman veiled with the veil of sincerity, that one enflamed by love and longing ..., lost in union with God, that one accepted by men as a second spotless Mary" (Schimmel 1975, 38). When once asked why she carried a torch in one hand and a pitcher of water in the other, she replied "I want to throw fire into Paradise and pour water into Hell so that these two veils disappear, and it becomes clear who worships God out of love, not out of fear of Hell or hope for Paradise" (Schmimmel 1975, 38f.). Rabi'a's all-consuming love of God provides an early model of the sort of love valorized by Sufism. Another early model was provided by al-Hallaj, who was tortured and then executed for having said "I am the Truth" or "true Reality," that is, God. Behind his apparent blasphemy was al-Hallaj's belief that the true lover of God should annihilate himself or herself so that God alone remains. He compares the lover of God to a moth attracted to a flame. The moth does not merely want its light or warmth but the flame itself, and so falls into it and is consumed by it with the result that the flame alone remains (Schimmel 1975, 69–72).

Later Sufis will insist that "Radical Love"[11] cannot be defined and since God's *essence* is love *God* cannot be defined. For "one can speak of something only through something more subtle and refined and there is nothing subtler than love. So what could ever express" it? (Sumnan, d. after 900, quoted in Safi 2018, 100). Or as Ibn Arabi asserted, love cannot be defined because "love has no definition through which its essence can be known. Rather it is given descriptive and verbal definitions, nothing more. Those who define love have not known it, those who have not tasted it by drinking it down have not known it, and those who say that they have been quenched by it have not known it, for

---

[11] A term coined by Omid Safi to designate the love prized by the great Islamic mystics – a love that "constantly spills over again and again, overflowing whatever cup seeks to contain it" (Safi 2018, xxi).

love is drinking without quenching" (Chittick 2008, 80). Yet as the quotation from Ibn Arabi illustrates, the fact that love can't be defined (that its essence can't be captured in words) doesn't imply that nothing true can be *said* of it. For consider the following two examples.

In the first place, the true lover eternally thirsts for God. Rumi compared the lovers in this respect to the sand "dunes which absorb the water as soon as it reaches them" (Schimmel 1975, 319). Or again, true lovers remove all the things from their path that God can give except God himself. For their love "is a purifying fire that burns away selfishness, greed, anger, ego, and leaves behind nothing but God" in our consciousness (Safi 2018, xxii). Jami, for example, urges us to cast all thoughts and imaginations from our heart until there abides with us neither consciousness of ourselves nor "even consciousness of such absence of consciousness" but God alone (Davis 1908, 55–6).

In the second place, the love in question "is not an emotion but a doing, a being, a burning . . . 'I was raw, then I burned, now I am on fire' [Rumi]" (Safi 2018, xxx). What is burnt up is everything other than God. "This world and the hereafter are the trash on the road to the Beloved. Until you remove the trash from the path you cannot arrive at the goal. What is not of God is no-thing. Whoever is not of God is no-one. Wherever you are with your notion of 'you,' that's hell. Wherever you discard your notion of 'you,' that's heaven" (Kharraz, abu Said, d. 899 or 890, quoted in Safi 2018, 31–2).

In surrendering to God, however, one surrenders to love, since love is God's essence, what he is in his own self. And because it *is* his essence, God's creative acts are necessarily expressions of God's love.

The tradition lists ninety-nine beautiful names or properties of God. "According to Ibn Arabi, these names are the creative possibilities latent in God," which "are called 'storehouses' in the Koranic verse 'There is nothing whose storehouses are not with us, but we send it down only in known measure' (15: 21)" (Chittick 2008, 93). Things come to be only when God "speaks" their names and they "hear (*sama'*)" them.[12]

Everything that exists is a product of "God's speaking" its name. The created universe in its entirety is thus a multiple and variegated expression of all the

---

[12] "The word *sama'* is also employed to mean 'listening to music' and by extension 'music'." (Moreover, because audition or music disposes the listener to movement or agitation it also involves a kind of dance [Chittick 2008, 96–7]), The dance and its accompanying music should not be taken too literally, however. "Dance" in the literal sense, for example, "has played a minor role in Sufism, even in the Mawlawiyya order where the whirling dance has had a certain importance" (Chittick 2008, 91). Music and dance in the most salient sense, however, are interior, in the advanced Sufi's heart. "In the words of [Ibn] Iraqi, 'The Song will never cease nor the dance come to an end, for all eternity, because the Beloved is infinite. Hence the lover hums: The moment I open my eyes I see your face. The instant I lend an ear I hear your voice.' So the lover continues to dance and move even though he may appear to be still" (Chittick 208, 120).

divine names. Each individual member of it is an expression of one or more of the divine names. Human beings, however, are intended to be an expression of *all* the divine names, and a "perfect human being" (a Sufi term) expresses all of them. As a consequence he or she is a microcosm of creation. There are therefore three divine books – the revealed book or Koran, the cosmos as a whole, and the "perfect human being," each in its own way expressing the wholeness of deity. And because God's essence is love, each of the divine books is also an expression of his love.

Even so, everything that is not God himself is only a *veil* of God. Even his light is a veil. "The only things we perceive through God's light are precisely the heavens and the earth, not God himself. When the Prophet was asked if he had seen God when he journeyed to him in his ascent . . . he replied, 'He is a light, how could I see him?'" (Chittick 2008, 181).[13]

Finally, our love of God is a gift of his grace. Our love of God thus begins and ends in him who is love itself. It can thus truly be said that God is both "the lover and the beloved, the seeker and the sought" (Chittick 2008, 80).

For a final example, consider the way in which Western medieval mystics combined the apophatic theology of Dionysius the Areopagite with the erotic imagery of the mystical marriage.

Pseudo-Dionysius's Platonism differs from that of Plotinus and other pagan Neo-Platonists in three important ways. For one thing, Dionysius does not accept Plotinus's doctrine of emanation. In his view, God creates out of nothing. "We do not receive our being from creatures higher than us in the hierarchies," who in turn, "receive their being from creatures at a still higher level." Dionysius appears to think that, on the contrary, an implication of the doctrine of creation *ex nihilo* is that each creature is immediately created by God. "Emanation," for Dionysius is "ultimately a matter of light, illumination and revelation, not of being." The higher levels mediate light or illumination and purifying knowledge to the lower levels but they do not mediate being (Louth 1981, 176).

In the second place, there are rather clear indications that Dionysius believes that salvation is ultimately a consequence of grace. The sensible "symbols" (Baptism, Eucharist, and Anointing) that the Christian uses to purify herself and begin her ascent to God owe their power to divine institution or decision, not to inherent fitness or natural sympathy as they do for pagan Neo-Platonic theurgists. Furthermore, in the ascent's final stage, the

---

[13] It is worth noting that a few texts ascribe cosmic significance to Mohammed himself. The *Quran* itself (21:107) says, "We send you Mohammed as a mercy to all the universes." And in a radical though disputed *Hadith Qudsi* (or Sacred Hadith) God goes so far as to say, "If not for you O Mohammed I would not have created the heavens" (Safi 2018, xl–xli).

Christian's soul is essentially passive, doing little or nothing other than holding herself open to the action of the divine energies. Plotinus's ontological system, on the other hand, can't accommodate the concept of grace. For first, the One is not a person. And second, union for Plotinus isn't an unmerited gift but a "natural occurrence." It is not a consequence of supernatural intervention but of the soul's own efforts and the ontological structure of reality that makes union possible (namely, [1] the fact that the soul is in permanent contact with the "intellect" [the world of intelligences or forms], which in turn is in permanent contact with the One, and [2] that everything tends to revert to it).

Finally, and perhaps most important, the Dionysian contemplative experiences God's love for her as well as her love for God. The soul unites with God in an ecstasy of love (*eros*), which Dionysius defines as "a power to effect a unity, an alliance, and a particular commingling of the Beautiful and the Good." The experience is ecstatic because one who is possessed by this love "belongs not to self but to the beloved." Thus, "the great Paul swept along by his yearning for God, and seized of its ecstatic power," said "It is no longer I who love Christ but Christ who lives in me." He "was truly a lover . . . and beside himself for God, possessing not his own life but the life of the One for whom he yearned." Similar language can be found in Plotinus. But what is inconceivable in Plotinus or any other pagan Neo-Platonist is that, in ecstasy, the soul encounters the divine power, *which comes to meet it*. Dionysius, on the other hand, believed that the soul's ecstatic love is met by God's ecstatic love. For "it must be said too that the very cause of the universe in the beautiful, good superabundance of its benign yearning for all is also carried outside himself in the loving care he has for all. He is as it were, beguiled by goodness, by love, and by yearning and is enticed away from his transcendent dwelling place and comes to abide within all things, and he does so by virtue of his supernatural and ecstatic capacity to remain nevertheless within himself" (Pseudo-Dionysius 1987, 81–83). Plotinus, on the other hand, denies that the One has any love or care for what proceeds from it. While love (a kind of "drunken" loving ecstasy) does appear to be a feature of the pagan Neo-Platonist mystic's experience of union, the love in question is the *love of the mystic for the One*; there is no indication that the mystic has a sense of *being loved by* the One. Dionysius thought that God transcends and is more than being and goodness (is "superbeing" and "supergoodness"). Although to the best of my knowledge he never explicitly says so, it seems that he is also committed to the claim that God transcends and is more than love as ordinarily understood (is superloving). There is nothing clearly comparable in pagan Neo-Platonism.

Dionysius's emphasis on love was developed further by his Western disciples. His *Celestial Hierarchy* "had ... noted that ... 'seraphim' means 'fire makers or carriers of warmth' while 'cherubim' means 'fullness of knowledge or carriers of wisdom' but he never identified the seraphic fire as the fire of love." Both John the Scot[14] and Hugh of St Victor do so. While John doesn't add "any references to charity or love" to his translation of the *Celestial Hierarchy*, his commentary on it "explains warmth as the warmth of charity, and fire as the ardor of love." The motion of the Seraphim around the One is "'super-burning' because the first hierarch of celestial powers burn above all who come after them in the love of the highest good." And Hugh agrees (Rorem 2009, 78–79).

Hugh's most important contribution to the Western affective Dionysian tradition, however, is his association of seraphic love with the bridal imagery of the *Song of Songs*. According to Hugh, the beloved of the *Song* "is loved more than understood ... Love (*dilectio*) surpasses knowledge and is greater than intelligence." In the divine bridal chamber, mortals and "angels surround by desire what they do not penetrate by intellect" (Hugh). Because "the bridal chamber of love is beyond the realm of knowing ... later authors can associate it with the darkness of unknowing, whether this be the cloud of M. Sinai or the dark night of the lovers' embrace" (Rorem 2009, 78–81).

For example, the anonymous author of the enormously influential *Cloud of Unknowing* says[15] that "by passing beyond yourself ... you shall be carried up in your affection, and above your understanding, to the substance beyond all substance, the radiance of the divine darkness," and exhorts the reader to "enter by affection into the darkness" that Moses entered through "exercising his affection alone" (Coolman 2004, 86–7). And similarly, "the last of the great Victorines," Thomas Gallus, claimed that Moses was "united to the intellectually unknown God through a union of love, which is affective or true cognition, a much better cognition than intellectual cognition" (Coolman 2009, 90f.). "For Gallus, while Dionysius offered a theoretical account of the soul's ascent to God, Solomon (in the *Song of Songs*) gives us the practice of the same mystical theology." The "ecstatic climax" of the soul's ascent merges "the love-sick night" of the *Song of Songs* "and the apophatic darkness of Dionysius's Moses" (Coolman 2009, 94). It is also worth noting that, for Gallus, while "in the darkness of seraphic union [with God] ... the soul lacks 'mental eyes,' that is reason and understanding," it *is* able to touch and taste the beloved. "This refreshment does not occur though a mirror, but through the experience of divine sweetness, because touch and taste are not experienced through

---

[14] The author of the first and highly influential Latin translation of the Dionysian corpus.

[15] In his Middle English paraphrase of the *Mystical Theology*, entitled *Denis's Hidden Theology*.

a mirror ... though vision is." And Gallus notes that while scripture says that no one can *see* God and live, it does *not* say that no one can touch or taste God and live (Coolman 2009, 94–5).

The affective Dionysian tradition not only infused the thought and practice of a number of the great Rhineland mystics such as Suso, Tauler, and Ruysbroeck but also deeply influenced Teresa of Avila, John of the Cross, and sixteenth-century Spanish mysticism more generally and, through them, many later Roman Catholic mystics as well. What is less commonly noted is the deep impact that a number of these mystics had on Protestant spiritual traditions. Luther was a great admirer of the *Theologia Germanica*,[16] for example. Johann Arndt was deeply influenced by Tauler, and Miguel de Molinos and Madame de Guyon were widely read by Pietists and other Protestants who emphasized the centrality of the interior life.

The nature of the Western affective Dionysian tradition will become clearer if we examine the views of at least one of them in more detail.

In his *Spiritual Espousals*, Jan van Ruysbroeck "speaks ... of a threefold division in the Christian life," namely, "the active, interior, and contemplative." The active life includes repentance, penitence, obedience to "God, the Holy Church, and [one's] own conscience in all things," and – most importantly – intending "God's glory in all [one's] works" (Ruysbroeck 1985, 155–6). My focus will be on the interior and contemplative lives, however.

In the second or interior division of the Christian life:

> God's interior stirring and touch makes us hunger and strive ... [And] the more there is of the touch, the more there is of the hunger and striving. This is a life of love at the highest level of [the soul's] activity ... God inclines himself toward us, and we are thereby touched in love; our spirit by means of God's activity and amorous power impels and inclines itself toward God, and thereby *God* is touched [my emphasis]. From these two movements there arises a struggle [or "storm"] of love, for in this most profound meeting ... spirit is wounded by love ... Our and God's spirit cast a radiant light upon one another and each reveals to the other its countenance ... Each demands of the other what it is, and each offers to the other and invites it to accept what it is. This makes these loving spirits lose themselves in one another. God's touch and his giving of himself together with our striving in loving and our giving ourselves in return ... sets love on a firm foundation. (Ruysbroeck 1985, 114–15)

The interior life is an expression of "active" love. But "active love prepares [us] for ... an '*essential* love' that is '*above*' all activity ... [Here] *the spirit becomes love itself*" (Mommaers 1995, 163, my emphases). As long as the spirit

---

[16] An anonymous fourteenth-century product of Rhineland mysticism.

continues to burn in love (as it does in the second stage) "it will be aware of distinction and difference between itself and God" when it examines itself. But when it is burnt up, "it is onefold and without distinction, and accordingly feels nothing but unity. Here a person becomes so possessed by love that he must forget both himself and God, and know nothing but love. In this way, the spirit is consumed in the fire of love, . . . and itself becomes love above all" works and "exercises of devotion"(Ruysbroeck 1985: 165).

What are we to make of this? Ruysbroeck sometimes says things that sound heretical. For example: "It is to be God with God, without intermediary or any element of otherness which could constitute an obstacle or impediment." Or again, "The soul becomes the very resplendence which it receives" (Ruysbroeck 1985: 146, 147) – which is reminiscent of the claims made by al-Hallaj. He also says that contemplatives "are transformed and become one with the same light with which they see and are seen" (Ruysbroeck 1985: 150), which is similar to the claims of Ibn Arabi.

But these statements of identity are phenomenological, not ontological. The "loving contemplative" temporarily loses awareness of his own separate identity. He "neither sees nor feels in the ground of his being, in which he is at rest, anything other than an incomprehensible light" (Ruysbroeck 1985: 147). There is no ontological identity, however, and those "who say that they themselves are Christ or God" are "foolish and perverse" (Ruysbroeck 1985: 229–30).

Precisely how, though, should union "without difference or distinction" be understood? Ruysbroeck describes it as "an eternal rest." This "rest is no longer in the contemplative's *own* deepest or essential being," however, "but rather in *God's* being (*wesen*) which is the superessential being (*overwesen*) of *all* beings, including the contemplative" herself (Ruysbroeck 1985: 30, my emphases). "There all exalted spirits are, in their superessential being one enjoyment, and one beatitude with God, without difference" (Ruysbroeck 1985: 266).[17] Ruysbroeck's exemplarism helps explain this.

"Colossians 1: 15–16 where Christ is spoken of as the image of the invisible God . . . in whom, through whom, and for whom all things have been created," and John 1: 1–4, which declares that "all things came to be through him" and that "all that came to be was alive with his life," provide the background for a doctrine of exemplarism that was developed by the Greek Fathers, Augustine, and by such later theologians as Anselm and Aquinas. Thomas Aquinas, for example, says that "all things 'are in God through their own intelligible natures,

---

[17] Note that Ruysbroeck says one in enjoyment and beatitude, not in ontological being. As he states in *The Mirror of Eternal Blessedness*, "whenever I write that we are one with God this is to be understood as a oneness in love and not in being or nature" (Ruysbroeck 1985, 247).

which in God is the same as the divine essence. Hence things that exist in God in that way *are* [my emphasis] the divine essence.'" Thus "creatures have not only their created being in the temporal order but also an eternal being in God, a being identical with God himself" (Ruysbroeck 1985; 19). Aquinas's idea if this: The Logos or Word includes the eternal exemplars of every temporal being. But given the divine simplicity, and the fact that the Logos or Word *is* God, my eternal or "intelligible being," too, is God; Ruysbroeck can thus say that "in this divine image [our intelligible being] all creatures have an eternal life apart from themselves in their eternal Exemplar ... It is to this eternal image and likeness that the Holy Trinity has created us. God therefore wills that we go out from ourselves into this divine light, supernaturally pursuing this image which is our own life and possessing it with him both actively and blissfully in a state of eternal blessedness" (Ruysbroeck 1985: 149). For even though *"all* creatures have this eternal life in God," contemplatives alone are able to "'*behold*' or *experience* it" Ruysbroeck, 1985: 20, my emphases.)

Love's Justification of Our Hope

As stated at the beginning of this section, our hopes aren't in vain if God loves us, and they are *most* secure if we are caught up in an intimate loving relationship with the object of our devotion. Rabi'a's all-consuming love of God is an example. The Vaishnavas think that one should model one's life on the companions of Vishnu by playing the role of his servants, companions, or lovers, but that the last is most important. Something similar is true of Christianity, where the God of grace and glory is often addressed as one's bridegroom and marriage is frequently thought to be the most appropriate image of the relation between God and his devotees.

Paul Tillich has argued that it is dangerously false to "define love by its emotional side" since this leads "necessarily to sentimental misinterpretations of love" such as a "chaotic self-surrender or [a] chaotic self-imposition," which fails to respect the otherness of the beloved (Tillich 1951, 79–80, 282). The ultimate reality that underlies the assertion that God is love (*agape*) is instead the fact that as the power of being overcoming nonbeing, "God works toward the fulfillment of every creature and toward the bringing into the unity of his life all who are separated and disrupted" (Tillich 1951, 151). In essence, Tillich more or less identifies God's love with the fact that Being itself is the ground of the world's existence, of the possibility of our overcoming our existential anxiety and estrangement, and the various realizations of those possibilities (Tillich 1951, 279–81).

Whether this is an adequate analysis of the peculiarly *theistic* understanding of love and grace is highly doubtful, however. For Shankara, for instance, or Plotinus could say something similar, namely, that the nirguna Brahman or the One is the ultimate ground of the world, of the possibility of our overcoming our estrangement, and of every realization of that possibility. Advaita Vedanta, for example, believes that the illusion of the space-time world is a joint product of the existence of the nirguna (propertyless) Brahman and our ignorance (*avidya*). Just as one can mistake a rope for a snake in the dark, so those entrapped in ignorance misperceive the Brahman without attributes as the space-time world. The existence of the nirguna Brahman, however, underlies both the possibility of our dispelling the ignorance that binds us to the illusion of the space-time world and of every realization of that possibility. But just as neither the nirguna Brahman nor the One *loves* us in any non-Pickwickian sense, so too it would seem neither does being itself.

Tillich's ontological love is thus an abstraction that bears little resemblance to the images of marital love, romantic love, and friendship that theists have deployed to express their relation to the religious ultimate. It is, at best, no more than a pale shadow of what we value in the most intense human love relationships and, by extension, in the love relationship between ourselves and God. Nor do views like Tillich's comport well with the Western apophatic tradition, which traces its roots to Pseudo-Dionysius and his early Western followers and has had a major impact on later Christian mystical theology. In traditions of this sort, "romantic" love isn't to be eliminated for the sake of something higher such as a perception of the "hidden Godhead," although it can be, and often is, *combined* with it. So-called romantic love is also central to more intense forms of *ordinary* monotheistic piety and devotion. Both the comparatively esoteric and the more popular forms of "romantic" love that we have discussed provide a more adequate account of the love valorized in the monotheistic traditions than the lean accounts provided by critics like Tillich.

But if the monotheist's relation to her God *actually is* like that described in these "romantic" traditions then her hope in God is as fully justified as it could possibly be.

The Traditions, Religious Exclusivism, and Love

There is a potential problem, however. The theistic traditions that valorize love typically believe that their love for God should be extended to God's creatures and, in particular, to one's fellow human beings. Yet in practice the love of the Christian or Muslim or Hindu monotheist doesn't always extend to the love of the religious other. Precisely how, then, should the adherents of the major monotheistic religions respond to the obvious diversity of those religions?

Only two responses are realistically possible[18] – exclusivism and inclusivism, both of which break down into two subcategories. Doctrinal exclusivists maintain that the central claims of one's "home religion" are true and the claims of "alien religions" that conflict with them are false.[19] Salvific exclusivists insist that salvation can only be found in their home religion. Doctrinal exclusivists may be salvific exclusivists as well, although many of them are not.

Doctrinal inclusivists are also salvific inclusivists. In their view, neither truth nor salvific efficacy is confined to one's home religion. Inclusivists do typically insist on the doctrinal and salvific superiority of the home religion, however. While doctrinal inclusivists are more inclined to believe that alien religions have much to teach us than are many doctrinal exclusivists, their positions aren't radically dissimilar. Both doctrinal exclusivists *and* doctrinal inclusivists agree that if one asserts a claim, he or she is, in consistency, bound to reject its denial as false, and neither is willing to abandon or radically modify the core claims of their home religions. The difference between them is at most a difference of degree. In the final analysis doctrinal inclusivism is neither more (nor less) than a somewhat more generous or open form of doctrinal exclusivism.

Relations between traditions are often far from irenic. A good example can be found in a nineteenth-century Sanskrit debate between the Christian John Muir and three Hindu pandits. The pandits' reaction to Christianity was almost entirely negative. It was accused of fostering "contempt for and abuse of animal life" because of its failure to acknowledge the role animals play in the reincarnation of souls, and its doctrine of creation *ex nihilo* was faulted because it seemed to directly implicate God in all the world's evils. Moreover, the pandits rejected Christianity's doctrines of original sin and forensic justification as illogical and unjust, and insisted that it was wrong to think that humanity's

---

[18] See my "Competing Religious Claims" (pp. 220–41, in *The Blackwell Guide to the Philosophy of Religion*, 2005, William E. Mann, ed. Malden MA & Oxford, UK: Blackwell Publishing) in which I argue that (a) there are real and significant theological differences between the major world religions, and that (b) the views of so-called "pluralists" like John Hick and Peter Byrne are not only fraught with internal difficulties but also could be reasonably rejected by educated, informed, and intelligent traditional monotheists. (For Hick's and Byrne's positions see, e.g., the former's *An Interpretation of Religion: Human Responses to the Transcendent*, 1989. New Haven and London: Yale University Press; and the latter's *Prolegomenon to Religious Pluralism: Reference and Reason in Religion*, 1995. London: Macmillan; New York: St. Martin's Press.)

[19] A "home religion is the one you belong to if you belong to one at all," and "alien religions . . . are any you do not belong to" (Griffiths 2001, xiv).

"basic defect" was moral rather than epistemological (Young 1981, 139). And so on.

Two things made it especially difficult for Muir and his adversaries to find common ground: the fact that the authority of the Vedas was assumed by the pandits to override any incompatible non-Vedic doctrine, and the fact that "in so far as [the pandits'] interpretations of Christianity enabled them to apprehend it accurately, Muir's exposition of that religion propounded little or nothing that hadn't been discussed at some time in Hinduism and rejected by the mainstream of orthodoxy" (Young 1981, 136). The debate between the Christian Muir and his Hindu opponents is an excellent illustration of the fact that strong attachments to one's own religious tradition are often (although not always) accompanied by a failure to take competing traditions seriously.

It is also worth noting that apparent irenicism is often *merely* apparent. Ibn Arabi, for instance, at one point says that "My heart takes on every form/ A pasture for gazelles/A cloister for monks/The idols' temple/A Ka'ba for the circling pilgrim/the Torah's tables, and the Qur'an's pages/I follow the religion of Love: Whichever way the caravan turns, I turn. This love is my religion, This is my faith" (Safi 2018, 121). It would be a major mistake, however, to infer that Ibn Arabi didn't think that Islam wasn't the true religion.

Yet isn't exclusivism irrational or in any case seriously wrongheaded? Why, after all, should Christianity, for example, be taken more seriously than Shri Vaishnavism or Islam, or Shri Vaishnavism or Islam more seriously than Christianity? For some Shri Vaishnavas, Christians, or Muslims are equally intelligent, well educated, and, not infrequently, fully cognizant of each other's views. They all appear, in short, to be the others' epistemic peers, and many have thought that "in cases of peer disagreement, one should give equal weight to the opinion of a peer and one's own opinion" (Kelly 2010, 112).[20] Yet just who *are* one's epistemic peers?

A necessary condition of two persons being peers with respect to an issue on which they disagree is that they share the same body of evidence. But in real-life cases, they often don't. As John Henry Newman pointed out, it is often "impossible to convey to others all the subtle strands of evidence one harbors or has harbored for one's opinion. One may have forgotten them, or in some cases they may not have been stored in one's memory in the first place. Failing

---

[20] Though, as Kelly points out, the trouble with so-called "conciliatory views" that instruct us to reduce our confidence in the face of peer disagreement is that they appear to be self-referentially incoherent since they undermine themselves. Because relevant epistemic peers disagree about the truth of conciliatorism, conciliatorism instructs us to abandon or at least significantly reduce our confidence in it. We could avoid this problem by excluding conciliatorism concerning the best or most reasonable response to peer disagreement from the scope of our principle, but doing so seems arbitrary.

to observe any counter examples to a certain hypothesis," for example, "may justify one's acceptance of it – at any rate if there is a high likelihood that one would observe such counterexamples if the hypothesis were false ... But the evidential 'omissions' that collectively constitute this (past) support tend not to be stored in memory and are not readily retrieved if one is asked to defend one's belief" (Goldman 2010, 211).

In other cases, such as medical diagnoses, cases in which "it is a very delicate matter to arrive at an all-things-considered judgment," and the like, "we are not considering relatively encapsulated tasks, and nor are we concerned with relatively basic cognitive judgments," but are, rather, "considering complicated expert judgments that are grounded in protracted experience in application of a diverse array of cognitive skills and capacities to the kind of question that is at issue." As a consequence, "there is a sense in which the two parties draw on very different bodies of evidence" (Oppy 2010, 197).

Then, too, even when two persons *appear* to share the same evidence, it isn't always clear that they really do. Suppose that I saw an accident and you didn't or that I remember what happened at an event at which you were absent. I can share my evidence with you by reporting to you what I saw or remembered, and "evidence of evidence is evidence" (Feldman 2007, 208). Yet consider a piece of evidence for proposition p, E1; and let E2 be evidence for E1. E2 may indeed be evidence for p. Does it necessarily follow, though, that E2 is as strong evidence for p as E1? (Suppose, for example, that E1 is my own memorial or perceptual experience, and that E2 is my report of E1.) If it doesn't, then E1 may neutralize or swamp the other's evidence for not-p even if his or her total evidence includes E2. For my perceptual *experiences* or *memories* have a power for me that mere *reports* of perceptions or memories necessarily lack. Because reports of one's experiences don't convey their "full evidential load," one's hearers justifiably accord a lower degree of confidence to p than the one who has had the experience justifiably accords to it (Goldman 2010, 210–12),

Furthermore, how one *takes* or *sizes up* the evidence is epistemically relevant even though it is not itself an additional *piece* of either public *or* private evidence. For example, when dealing with value-laden matters, whether or not one finds an argument or body of evidence convincing is at least partly a function of what William James called our "passional nature" or "temperament" – our hopes and fears, desires and aversions, intimations, longings, and the like, and these vary from one person to another. These yearnings, fears, and the like don't *add* anything to one's evidence, but they clearly affect how one *reads* it.

Moreover, as Richard Fumerton points out, while I have direct access to my own intellectual processing, I have no direct access to the intellectual processing of those with whom I disagree. In cases where I and my apparent peer disagree even though we are more or less equally intelligent, informed, and the like, I have no good reason to think that he or she is processing the evidence better than, or even as well as, I am. Where philosophers or theologians disagree, for example, epistemic modesty is no doubt in order, but where I am "reasonably confident" that my views are correct and can detect no flaws in my intellectual processing, my comparative lack of acquaintance with the inner processing of my opponent justifies my standing firm. For as Newman also pointed out, "in the final analysis there is really no alternative to the egocentric perspective" (Fumerton 2010, 106).

This does not imply that one is immune from error, of course, for one has higher-order evidence of one's own fallibility. But "to acknowledge that higher-order considerations [of this sort] make *some* difference" doesn't commit one to thinking "that they make *all* the difference ... When one possesses what is in fact" a correct assessment of the evidence "that one correctly recognizes as such one possesses an extremely strong piece of evidence" that "[i]sn't easily washed away by the fact" that one's colleagues fail to appreciate it. It is true that your colleagues "might feel just as confident that" your reasoning is flawed "as you might feel that it is sound." But this is hardly decisive since "in general when one reasons badly, one's phenomenology" can be indistinguishable from one's phenomenology "when one reasons impeccably" (Kelly 2010, 135–50)

So how does this bear on religious disputes? John Cobb had argued that entering dialogue with a prior commitment to the truth of one's home religion is unacceptably arrogant since it antecedently disqualifies the other religions when "in every fiber of [their] being" they refuse "to be disqualified" (Cobb 1982, 30–1). Yet notice that precisely the same charge can be leveled at even the most irenic *philosophical* exclusivists.

Consider, for example, disputes between materialism or physicalism,[21] on the one hand, and Platonic idealists, on the other, or between determinists and indeterminists, or Kantian moralists and consequentialists. The analogy is important, for philosophical disputes of this sort are paradigmatic examples of dialogues typically marked by mutual respect, a willingness to learn, to make and respond to criticism, and (in principle at least) to abandon one's view if the argument demands it. Furthermore, dialogue of this sort is essential to the practice of philosophy. Something is lacking if compatibilists, for example,

---

[21] The distinction is roughly this. Adherents of the former believe that matter alone is fundamentally real. Adherents of the latter think reality can be reduced to the basic elements (e.g., quarks and the like) of our most advanced physics.

talk only to each other. And this remains true even if compatibilists are pretty good at envisaging incompatibilist alternatives and objections to their own positions. For other things being equal (intelligence, knowledge, etc.), alternatives and criticism are most effectively presented and pressed home by those who subscribe to them.

Yet is there any reason to expect that, as a result of such dialogue, the positions of either member of one of these pairs of opposed philosophical views will be radically transformed and not merely transformed around the edges? Is there any reason to think that either one of them *should* be? And if so, how? In the face of unresolved disagreements, the equal weight view would arguably require agnosticism or skepticism. Agnosticism or skepticism doesn't transform the opposed positions, however; they abandon them. And a third position combining the insights of determinism, say, and indeterminism is hard to imagine. (Compatibilism is still a form of determinism, and a two-level or noumenal-phenomenal view like Kant's is, if coherent at all, still indeterminist.) Furthermore, in cases in which the competing positions are clearly incompatible if taken at face value, finding a significant common core or modifying the competing positions in a way that eliminates the inconsistency without essentially abandoning at least one of them will seldom be a plausible option. Is there any reason to think, then, that at the end of the dialogue between (e.g.) determinists and indeterminists, most adherents of one of these positions won't (quite properly, given their reasons, perspective, and the like) continue to judge the other opinion to be false, that is, remain philosophical doctrinal exclusivists?

If there isn't, then why balk at *religious* doctrinal exclusivism? Perhaps the two sorts of disagreement are relevantly different. But if so, how? One possible outcome of philosophical disagreement is suspension of judgment. A similar move in the case of theological disagreement would involve abandoning one's faith stance and one might think that this is problematic in a way that suspending judgment on a purely philosophical issue is not. But any difference here is at best one of degree. Not all theological issues carry heavy existential freight, and many philosophical issues do. William James, for example, confessed that he desperately needed to believe in the freedom of his will, while Plato thought that materialism had deleterious moral and spiritual consequences. It is also true that religious intolerance can have horrendous consequences, whereas entrenched positions on the status of universals (for example) do not. But the differences here can be exaggerated. That doctrinal religious exclusivism is often combined with salvific inclusivism and a commitment to liberal social and political values suggests that doctrinal religious exclusivism by itself doesn't necessarily do so.

On the other hand, philosophical views, too, can have problematic social and political consequences. (Witness the role played by Rousseau's *Social Contract* in the excesses of the French Revolution, for instance, or the questionable impact of consequentialism on contemporary bureaucratic institutions.)

The upshot is that it is at least arguable that the most intellectually honest response to the doctrinal diversity of the world's religions is either agnosticism or skepticism, or (more irenically) a suitably modest form of doctrinal exclusivism.

But what attitude should the devout Christian, for example, take toward her religious others? The fact that they dismiss us if they do, or don't love us if they don't, doesn't justify us in dismissing or not loving *them*. On the contrary, if (as Kierkegaard and others have argued) God is love and one truly loves God, one must love those *whom* he loves. Moreover, one's love must be *genuine*. (While some Christian fundamentalists, for example, *profess* to love their opponents, their behavior sometimes suggests that they neither respect nor genuinely love them.)

One of the more interesting and irenic attempts to dissolve the problem of the religious other is Karl Rahner's. His "Christianity and the Non-Christian Religions" states four theses. The first is that Christianity rests on "God's free self-revelation" in Christ's sacrificial death and resurrection, and "understands itself as the absolute religion intended for all men, which cannot recognize any religions beside itself as of equal right" (Rahner 1966, 118).

His second and third theses are the most interesting and also the most controversial. The second is this: "Until the moment when the gospel really enters into the historical situation of an individual,[22] a non-Christian religion," while containing errors, may also contain "supernatural elements arising out of the grace which is given to men as a gratuitous gift *on account of Christ*" (Rahner 1966, 121, my emphasis).

For though it is true both that "there is no salvation apart from Christ" and that God "has seriously intended this salvation for all men," it is also true that it is "quite unthinkable that man being what he is could actually achieve" a proper relationship to God's offer of grace "in an absolutely private interior reality . . . outside of the actual religious bodies which offer themselves to him in the

---

[22] Roughly, until Christianity (in William James's words) is a "live option," as it is not for most Muslims and Vaishnavas, for example. A choice is living, in James's sense, if each alternative "appears as a real possibility to whom it is proposed" – that is, if one has some inclination to believe and thus act on it (*The Will to Believe and Other Essays in Popular Philosophy*, 1896, reprint, New York: Dover, 1956, p. 2).

environment in which he lives." Rahner's conclusion is that because Christianity isn't a live option for most of the devout of other faiths and since God can only be accessed through the practice of some concrete religion or other, God's grace in Christ is bestowed upon them *through* their devout practice of their religions (Rahner 1966, 123, 128).

If this is so (and this is Rahner's third thesis), a Christian should not treat a "member of an extra-Christian religion as a mere non-Christian . . . but as an *anonymous* Christian," namely a man or woman who has in effect experienced the grace that God has made available through Christ in the non-Christian religion to which he or she belongs (Rahner 1966, 131–2).

Finally (thesis four) while the devout Christian may rightfully hope that the "anonymous Christian" will convert to Christianity itself, she must never forget that "God is greater than man *and the Church*" (Rahner 1966, 134, my emphasis).

Yet by parity of reason, couldn't a devout and learned Muslim after the pattern of Ibn Arabi, for example, argue that at least some Christians are "anonymous Muslims"? I think that he or she could but am not sure that this poses a major difficulty for Rahner's general position.

Christians and anonymous Christians don't share precisely the same body of evidence, since their experiences and the way they cognitively process them presumably differ. It may nonetheless be true that given the evidence that each possesses and their methods of cognitive processing that evidence, both the Christian and the anonymous Christian are epistemically entitled to their respective positions. And note also that even if the Christian's overall evidence is in fact superior to that of a Muslim, say, or a Shri Vaishnava, it might *not* be superior in every respect – in which case the former can learn from the latter.

Similarly, Muslims, too, and anonymous Muslims wouldn't share precisely the same body of evidence since their experiences and the way they cognitively process them would presumably differ as well. It may nevertheless be true that given the evidence at the disposal of each and their diverse methods of cognitively processing that evidence, both the Muslim and the anonymous Muslim may be epistemically entitled to their distinctive positions. And once again, even if the Muslim's overall evidence is in fact superior to that of either the Christian or the anonymous Muslim, it might not be superior to the latter in every respect – in which case the former can learn from the latter.

Still, isn't the Christian's or Muslim's insistence on the overall epistemic superiority of their positions an unattractive form of exclusivism?

In discussing Karl Barth's claim that all religions except Christianity are products of human pride and self-interest, Keith Ward comments that

> The belief that everyone else's revelation is [at least partly] incorrect and only one's own is [fully] true is a particularly clear example of human pride and self-interest ... [One] has an interest in thinking one's religion is the only [fully] true one [since] it enables one to ... bask in the superiority of one's own possession of the truth. One may claim that [one possesses the truth] by the grace of God alone – but this only makes the element of human pride more pronounced since one is now asserting that grace is only [fully] possessed by oneself. One can hardly get more proud, more self-righteous, and more short-sighted than that. (Ward 1994, 17)

Ward goes on to say that "Exclusivists like Barth are like the self-righteous Pharisee who thanks God that he is not as other people are (Luke 18: 9–14)." And no doubt this is a rather too common failing. Yet it is important to note that the critics of the more irenic religious exclusivists are often guilty of a similar arrogance.

Puritan divines argued that we should not question the profession of fellow Christians unless their behavior notoriously belied it. To do so was to sin against charity. Christian or Muslim exclusivists who accuse others of moral and spiritual blindness *but also their critics* should at least wonder whether their accusations, too, are rooted in a lack of love as well as in the force of their arguments and superior insight, and whether their own blindness therefore (while different) is any less free from fault.

Bibliography

Alston, William P. (1989). *Divine Nature and Human Language: Essays in Philosophical Theology*. Ithaca, NY: Cornell University Press.

Anselm (1965). *Anselm's Proslogion with a Reply on Behalf of the Fool by Gaunilo, and the Author's Reply to Gaunilo*. Translated by with an introduction and philosophical commentary by M. J. Charlesworth. Oxford: Clarendon Press.

Aquinas, Thomas (1947). *The Summa Theologica*, vol. 2. Translated by Fathers of the English Dominican Provence. New York: Benziger Bros.

Augustine (1953). *Enchiridion or Manual to Laurentius concerning Faith, Hope, and Charity*. London: S. P. C. K.

Azrael of Gerona (1986). Explanation of the Ten Sefirot. In Joseph Dan, ed., *The Early Kabbalah*. New York: Paulist Press, pp. 89–96.

Chittick, William C. (2000). *Sufism: A Beginner's Guide*. Oxford: One World Publications.

Chrysostom (1984). *On the Incomprehensible Nature of God*. Translated by Paul W. Harkins, Fathers of the Church. Washington: The Catholic University of America Press.

Coolman, Boyd Taylor (2009).The Medieval Affective Dionysian Tradition. In S. Coakley and C. M. Stang, eds., *Re-Thinking Dionysius the Areopagite*. Chichester: Wiley-Blackwell, pp. 83–102.

Cudworth, Ralph (1678). *The True Intellectual System of the Universe*, vol. 1. London: Richard Royston; reprinted New York: Garland, 1978.

Dasgupta, Surendranath (1955). *A History of Indian Philosophy*, vol. 3. Cambridge: Cambridge University Press.

Davis, Frederick Hedland (1918). *The Persian Mystics: Jami*. London: John Murray. Reprinted Cosimo Classics, New York 2007.

Dionysius the Areopagite (Pseudo-Dionysius) (1957). *The Divine Names and the Mystical Theology*. Translated by C. E. Rolt. London: Macmillan.

(1987). *Pseudo-Dionysius: The Complete Works*. Mahwah, NJ: Paulist Press.

Epstein, Isidore (1959). *Judaism: A Historical Presentation*. London: Penguin Books.

Epstein, Isidore (1971). *Judaism: A Historical Presentation*. Harmondsworth, Middlesex: Penguin Books.

Feldman, Richard (2007). Reasonable Religious Disagreements. In Louise Anthony, ed. *Philosophers without Gods: Meditations on Atheism and the Secular Life*. New York: Oxford University Press.

Fumerton, Richard (2010). You Can't Trust Philosophers. In Richard Feldman and Ted A. Warfield, eds., *Disagreement*. New York: Oxford University Press, pp. 91–110.

Gellman, Jerome (2013). The God of the Jews and the Jewish God. In C. Taliaferro, V. S. Harrison, and S. Goetz, eds., *The Routledge Companion to Theism*. New York and Abingdon, Oxon: Routledge, pp. 38–53.

Goldman, Alvin I. (2010). Epistemic Relativism and Reasonable Disagreement. In Richard Feldman and Ted A. Warfield, eds. *Disagreement*. New York: Oxford University Press, pp. 187–215.

Griffiths, Paul J. (1994). *On Being Buddha: The Classical Doctrine of Buddhahood*. Albany: State University of New York Press.

(2001). *Problems of Religious Diversity*. Malden, MA and Oxford: Blackwell.

Haberman, David L. (1988). *Action as a Way of Salvation: A Study of Raganuga Bhakti Sadhana*. Oxford and New York: Oxford University Press.

Kelly, Thomas (2010). Peer Disagreement and Higher Order Evidence. In Richard Feldman and Ted A. Warfield, eds., *Disagreement*. Oxford University Press, pp. 113–74.

Kierkegaard, Søren (1962). *Works of Love. Some Christian Reflections in the Form of Discourses.* Translated by Howard and Edna Hong. New York: Harper Torchbooks.

Kumar, P. Pratap (1997). *The Goddess Laksmi: The Divine Consort in the South Indian Vaisnava Tradition*. Atlanta, GA: Scholars Press.

Lipner, Julius (1986). *The Face of Truth: A Study of Meaning and Metaphysics in the Vedantic Theology of Ramanuja*. Albany: State University of New York Press.

Louth, Andrew (1981). *The Origins of the Christian Mystical Tradition from Plato to Denis*. Oxford: Clarendon Press.

Marcel, Gabriel (1952). *Homo Viator: Introduction to the Metaphysics of Hope*. Translated by Emma Crawford. New York: Harper Torchbooks.

Mierav, Ariel (2009). The Nature of Hope. *Ratio* 22 (2), 216–33.

Moltmann, Jurgen (1967, 1993). *Theology of Hope: On the Grounds and the Implications of a Christian Eschatology*. London: SCM Press; Minneapolis: Fortress Press.

Mommaers, Paul (1995). Mystically One with God. In Paul Mommears and Jan Van Bragt, eds., *Mysticism, Buddhist and Christian: Encounters with Jan Van Ruusbroec*. New York: Crossroad, pp. 156–77.

Oppy, Graham (2010). Disagreement. *International Journal for Philosophy of Religion* 68: 183–99.

Rahner, Karl (1966). Christianity and the Non-Christian Religions. *Theological Investigations*, vol. 5. London: Darton, Longman & Todd; Baltimore: Helicon Press. pp. 115–34.

(1974). The Concept of Mystery in Catholic Theology. *Theological Investigations*, vol. 4. New York: Seabury, pp. 36–73.

Ramanuja (1956). *Vedarthasamgrahha*. Translated by S. S. Raghavachar. Mysore: Sri Ramakrishna Ashrama.

(1962). *The Vedanta Sutras with the Commentary by Ramanuja*. Translated by George Thibaut. Delhi: Motilal Banarsidass.

Rorem, Paul (2009). The Early Latin Dionysius: Eriugena and Hugh of St. Victor. In S. Coakley and C. M. Stang, eds., *Rethinking Dionysius the Areopagite*. Chichester: Wiley-Blackwell, pp. 71–84.

Rowe, William L. (1968). *Religious Symbols and God: A Philosophical Study of Tillich's Theology*. Chicago: University of Chicago Press.

Ruysbroeck, Jan (1985). *John Ruusbroec: The Spiritual Espousals and Other Works*. Translated by with Introduction, James A. Wiseman. Mahwah, NJ: Paulist Press.

Safi, Omid (2018). *Radical Love: Teachings from the Islamic Mystical Tradition*. Translated and edited by Omid Safi. New Haven and London: Yale University Press.

Sarma, Deepak (2003). *An Introduction to Madhva Vedanta*. Aldershot, Hampshire and Burlington, VT: Ashgate.

Schimmel, Annemarie (1975). *Mystical Dimensions of Islam*. Chapel Hill: University of North Carolina Press.

Scholem, Gershom G. (1946). *Major Trends in Jewish Mysticism*. New York: Schocken.

(1987). *Origins of the Kabbalah*. Princeton, NJ: Princeton University Press.

Schweig, Graham M. (2014). The Upadesamrtam of Rupa Gosvami: A Concise Teaching on Essential Practices of Krsna *Bhakti*. In Ravi N. Gupta, ed., *Caitanya Vaishnava Philosophy: Tradition, Reason and Devotion*. Aldershot, Hampshire and Burlington VT: Ashgate, pp. 163–74.

Shankara (1962). *The Vedanta Sutras of Badarayana with the Commentary by Sankara*. Translated by George Thibaut. New York: Dover.

(1970). *Shankara's Crest Jewel of Discrimination*. Translated by Swami Prabhavananda. New York: Mentor Books.

Tillich, Paul (1951). *Systematic Theology*, vol. 1. Chicago: University of Chicago Press.

(1957), *Dynamics of Faith*. New York: Harper.

Tinder, Glen (1999). *The Fabric of Hope: An Essay*. Grand Rapids, MI and Cambridge, UK: William B. Eerdmans.

Ward, Keith (1994). *Religion and Revelation: A Theology of Revelation in the World's Religions*. Oxford: Clarendon Press.

Williams, Paul (1989). *Mahayana Buddhism: The Doctrinal Foundations*. London and New York: Routledge.

Young, Richard Fox (1981). *Resistant Hinduism: Sanskrit Sources on Anti-Christian Apologetics in Early Nineteenth Century India*. Vienna: Publications of the De Nobili Research Library.

Cambridge Elements ☰

Religion and Monotheism

Paul K. Moser
Loyola University Chicago
Paul K. Moser is Professor of Philosophy at Loyola University Chicago. He is the author of *The God Relationship*; *The Elusive God* (winner of national book award from the Jesuit Honor Society); *The Evidence for God*; *The Severity of God*; *Knowledge and Evidence* (all Cambridge University Press); and *Philosophy after Objectivity* (Oxford University Press); co-author of *Theory of Knowledge* (Oxford University Press); editor of *Jesus and Philosophy* (Cambridge University Press) and *The Oxford Handbook of Epistemology* (Oxford University Press); co-editor of *The Wisdom of the Christian Faith* (Cambridge University Press). He is the co-editor with Chad Meister of the book series *Cambridge Studies in Religion, Philosophy, and Society.*

Chad Meister
Bethel University
Chad Meister is Professor of Philosophy and Theology and Department Chair at Bethel College. He is the author of *Introducing Philosophy of Religion* (Routledge, 2009), *Christian Thought: A Historical Introduction*, 2nd edition (Routledge, 2017), and *Evil: A Guide for the Perplexed*, 2nd edition (Bloomsbury, 2018). He has edited or co-edited the following: *The Oxford Handbook of Religious Diversity* (Oxford University Press, 2010), *Debating Christian Theism* (Oxford University Press, 2011), with Paul Moser, *The Cambridge Companion to the Problem of Evil* (Cambridge University Press, 2017), and with Charles Taliaferro, *The History of Evil* (Routledge 2018, in six volumes).

About the Series
This Cambridge Elements series publishes original concise volumes on monotheism and its significance. Monotheism has occupied inquirers since the time of the Biblical patriarchs, and it continues to attract interdisciplinary academic work today. Engaging, current, and concise, the Elements benefit teachers, researchers, and advanced students in religious studies, Biblical studies, theology, philosophy of religion, and related fields.

Cambridge Elements ☰

Religion and Monotheism

Elements in the Series

Buddhism and Monotheism
Peter Harvey

Monotheism and the Meaning of Life
T. J. Mawson

Monotheism and Contemporary Atheism
Michael Ruse

Monotheism and Hope in God
William J. Wainwright

A full series listing is available at: www.cambridge.org/er&m